# Winning Strategies for Success

D1666462

# WINNING STRATEGIES

## FOR SUCCESS

### SUCCEEDING IN BUSINESS IN ANY MARKET

1. Edition 2024

Copyright@ 2024 by
Brian Tracy Publishing
Progrowth For Business Solutions
Dubai, United Arab Emirates

**Winning Strategies For Success**
**Succeeding In Business In Any Market Volume III**

International Publisher
Zaki International GmbH
Schonnebeckhöfe 6
45309 Essen
Germany

**ISBN Hardcover:**    978-3-98918-015-4
**ISBN Paperback:**    978-3-98918-016-1
**ISBN eBook:**        978-3-98918-017-8

**Consulting & project management:**
"Mr. Bestseller" Hartmut Paschke, www.hartmutpaschke.com

**Disclaimer**
All advice in this book has been carefully considered and reviewed by the author and publisher. However, no guarantee can be given. Therefore, the author and publisher shall not be liable for any personal, property or financial damages.

For questions and suggestions:
**info@progrowth.ae**

*Vivian Weris stands as a remarkable figure in the entrepreneurial and empowerment arenas, dedicating her life to fostering strength and self-confidence in women around the globe. Her journey from overcoming personal hardships to founding her own company encapsulates a story of resilience, determination, and transformation. Through her innovative use of neuropsychological tools and a passion-driven approach, Vivian has become a beacon of hope for women seeking to reclaim their power and achieve fulfillment in both life and business. Vivian Weris actively creates a legacy of change, encouraging women to rise above their circumstances and flourish.*

Brian Tracy
Author, Speaker, Consultant

# CONTENTS

# FOREWORD
# BRIAN TRACY

As I reflect on the journey that led to the creation of this third volume in our "Succeeding in Business in Any Market" series named as "Winning Strategies for Success", my heart is filled with a deep sense of gratitude and anticipation. It has been a privilege to work once again with my esteemed colleague, Medhat Zaki, and a remarkable group of co-authors whose commitment to excellence continues to inspire me.

The success of our previous volumes has reinforced an important truth: the combined wisdom of diverse experiences is a powerful catalyst for transformation and growth. This latest edition builds on that foundation, delving deeper into the strategies and disciplines essential to navigating the complexities of today's business environment.

Our world is in a constant state of flux, marked by rapid advances in technology, shifts in consumer behavior and unpredictable economic landscapes. Yet in the midst of these challenges, the principles of success remain steadfast. It is our adaptability, our thirst for knowledge and our commitment to innovation that determine our ability to thrive.

In this volume, we have curated a collection of insights from leaders across industries, each sharing their unique perspective on achieving success. From groundbreaking strategies to timeless wisdom, these chapters provide a roadmap for those who want to leave an indelible mark on their field.

I have always maintained that success is not the result of chance, but the culmination of deliberate action, guided by a clear vision and unwavering perseverance. This book is a testament to that belief, providing not only the inspiration but also the practical knowledge you need to excel in any market.

To our distinguished co-authors, I extend my deepest appreciation for your contributions. Your experiences, challenges, and triumphs serve as beacons of possibility for us all. And to you, our readers, I offer this third volume as a tool and an ally in your journey to success.

Let us face the challenges ahead together, armed with the knowledge and insights contained within these pages. Remember, the road to greatness is often unpaved and uncertain, but with the right guidance and mindset, the possibilities are limitless.

Success awaits those who dare to pursue it with passion and purpose. Let this book be your guide on the journey ahead. The future is not just something you experience—it is something you create.

With warm regards and best wishes for your continued success,

Brian Tracy

# FOREWORD
# MEDHAT ZAKI

Dear reader,

As we begin the third volume of our acclaimed series, "Winning Strategies for Success", I find myself reflecting on the journey that has brought us here. My name is Medhat Zaki, and I'm delighted to welcome you to this latest collection of insights and methods designed to catapult you to unparalleled business success.

Previous volumes in our series have resonated with readers around the world, combining the entrepreneurial spirit with useful knowledge and profound wisdom from leaders in a wide range of industries. This new edition builds on that legacy by delving deeper into the themes of invention, tenacity and strategic insight. Our co-authors, a wide range of experts from different professions, have over 500 years of combined experience. Their stories are more than just success stories; they are blueprints for making an unforgettable impact on any endeavour, personal or professional.

My journey from a humble background in Egypt to being an entrepreneur in Germany has been one of constant learning, resilience and, most importantly, sharing. Giving back is at the heart of our series. Meeting Brian Tracy changed my perspective on business and life and instilled in me the belief that wisdom is the greatest legacy one can leave. Our collaboration, combined with the contributions of our esteemed co-authors, demonstrates the potential of collective insights and shared experiences.

This third book provides a roadmap for individuals navigating the ever-changing difficulties of the business world. More than just a repository of knowledge, it is also a source of encouragement and a reminder that success is possible regardless of market conditions. Within these pages, you will discover a treasure trove of methods forged in the fires of real-world application and honed through the lens of experience and success.

Our ever-changing world demands adaptability, insight, and a commitment to continuous improvement. The stories and lessons in this collection reflect these realities. They have been hand-picked to inspire, educate and guide you to your business goals and beyond. As you move through the chapters, each with its own unique perspective and hard-earned wisdom, I encourage you to draw freely from this pool of knowledge and apply these concepts to forge your own path to success.

The journey of business and personal development is an ongoing one, defined by our choices, our actions, and the people we choose to listen to and learn from. The name of our series, "Succeeding in Business in Any Market", is more than a title; it's a promise—a commitment to deliver key insights that stand the test of time and market volatility.

I am very pleased with what we have achieved with this series and the community we have created around these shared values of tenacity, wisdom and shared success. As you begin or continue your journey, may this volume be your faithful companion, revealing possibilities and inspiring a bold vision for the future.

Welcome back to a study of greatness in business and beyond. May the pages of this third book serve as stepping stones on your journey to unprecedented success.

With deep respect and best wishes for your success,

Medhat Zaki

# Brian Tracy

Brian Tracy is chairman and CEO of Brian Tracy International, a company specializing in the training and development of individuals and organizations. Brian's goal is to help you achieve your personal and business goals faster and easier than you ever imagined. Brian Tracy has consulted for more than 1,000 companies and addressed more than 5,000,000 people in 5,000 talks and seminars throughout the US, Canada, and 70 other countries worldwide. He has studied, researched, written, and spoken for 30 years in the fields of economics, history, business, philosophy, and psychology. He is the top-selling author of over 70 books that have been translated into dozens of languages.

He speaks to corporate and public audiences on the subjects of Personal and Professional Development, including the executives and staff of many of America's largest corporations. His exciting talks and seminars on Leadership, Selling, Self-Esteem, Goals, Strategy, Creativity, and Success Psychology bring about immediate changes and long-term results.

Prior to founding his company, Brian Tracy International, Brian was the Chief Operating Officer of a $265 million dollar development company. He has had successful careers in sales and marketing, investments, real estate development, and syndication, importation, distribution, and management consulting. He has conducted high-level consulting assignments with several billion-dollar-plus corporations in strategic planning and organizational development. He is active in community and national affairs and is the President of three companies headquartered in Solana Beach, California.

SCAN ME

# Chapter 1

# THE 7 KEYS TO EXPONENTIAL SUCCESS

**Brian Tracy**

Your ability to set goals and make plans for their accomplishment is the "master skill" of success. The development of this ability and your making it a lifelong habit will do more to assure high success and achievement than any other skill you can possibly learn.

As with anything, you only own the process of goal setting by learning it and then by applying it over and over for yourself until it becomes automatic, like breathing in and breathing out. Your behavioral goal must be to become a continuous goal setter. You must become so clear and focused about what it is you want that you are doing things that move you toward your goals every minute of every day.

**Intelligence and Success**

Not long ago, 1500 successful men and women were interviewed to find out what specific qualities they felt they had that had enabled them to rise above 99% of the people in society. One of the qualities they identified was that of "intelligence." But when they were pressed for the definition of intelligence, most of the respondents agreed that intelligence was more a "way of acting" than it was IQ or grades in school.

They concluded that people who were successful acted intelligently. People who were unsuccessful acted unintelligently. Many people from the best colleges with high levels of IQ engaged in unintelligent behaviors. And many people with limited beginnings and blessings engaged in very intelligent behaviors.

So the question then became, "What is, by definition, an intelligent behavior?"

The answer is simple. An intelligent behavior is anything that you do that moves you in the direction of something that you have decided that you want for yourself. An unintelligent or "stupid" behavior is anything that you do that moves you away from something that you have decided that you want.

For example, if you decide that one of your goals is excellent health and fitness, everything you do to attain that goal is intelligent. Everything that you do, or neglect to do, that takes away from your health and fitness, is, by your own definition, a stupid act.

If your goal is to enjoy a high income and become financially independent, everything you do that enables you to increase your personal value and build up your financial resources is intelligent. Any time you do something that moves you away from financial independence, or even when you do something that does not move you toward financial independence, you are behaving unintelligently — by your own definition of what you really want.

## Become More Intelligent

Here is a remarkable discovery: Your intelligence is malleable over about 25 IQ points. This means that you can increase your IQ by using your mind better. You can become smarter by working on your mental muscles, just as you can become physically stronger by working on your physical muscles. And with clear, specific goals that you are working toward each day, you will find yourself acting more and more intelligently in everything you do.

Perhaps one of the most important discoveries of the last 100 years is that you have an automatic, cybernetic, goal-achieving mechanism built into your brain. Human beings are the only creatures on earth that have this particular capacity. Because of this capability, you automatically achieve the goals that you have set for yourself, whatever they are.

This "success mechanism" works night and day, consciously and unconsciously. It both drives you and motivates you toward achieving the goals you have set for yourself. It is almost like a light switch. Once you turn it on, it stays on until you do something to turn it off.

## Activate Your Success Mechanism

The great problem with most people is that their automatic goal setting mechanism switch is not turned on. Or, if it is turned on, it is focused on achieving goals of limited importance and value. When many people come into work in the morning, their primary goal is to decide what they are going to do at lunchtime. In the afternoon, their primary goal is to decide what they are going to watch on television that evening. For the weekend, their primary goal is how they will enjoy themselves and pass the time. When they pick up their smartphone, their primary goal is to read every sports score that has been accumulated in the nation in the past 24 hours or lose minutes and hours on social media. When they go shopping, their primary goal is to spend everything they have and everything they can charge on credit. They are more concerned with tension relieving than with goal achieving.

## Everything Counts

Here is one of the most important of all success principles: "Everything counts!"

Everything you do adds up or takes away. Everything either helps or hurts. Everything action, or inaction, either moves you toward your goals or moves you away from them. Nothing is neutral. Everything counts.

You either win the game of life by deliberate design and by definite activities on your part, or you lose the game of life by default, by not playing the game in the first place. You lose the game of life if you fail to switch on your success mechanism and keep it on until you achieve the goals you set for yourself.

Each person also has a "failure mechanism" built into his or her subconscious mind. This failure mechanism is often seen when people seek the fastest and easiest way to get the things they want. Most people follow the line of least resistance. They prefer to do what is fun and easy in the short term rather than what is hard and necessary to assure better results in the long term.

Every morning, when you arise, you are faced with a choice. Do you do what is fun and easy, or do you do what is hard and necessary? Do you get up and get yourself ready for the day, or do you get up and scroll through your social media accounts?

**Think About the Consequences**

The best way to analyze the importance and value of your behaviors is to think in terms of long-term potential consequences. If a behavior is valuable and important, it is something that can have significant consequences in your life. If a behavior is unimportant and irrelevant, it is something that has no consequences at all.

For example, if you drink coffee, stare endlessly at your phone and watch television, these behaviors will have no consequences for your health, happiness and prosperity, except perhaps negative ones. You can engage in these time-wasting activities for hours. You can become one of the most skillful social media scrollers, television watchers and coffee drinkers in the history of the American republic, and it will have absolutely zero effect on your future. Therefore, by definition, these are unimportant, low-value behaviors because they have no helpful consequences.

On the other hand, getting up, exercising, and reading 30–60 minutes each morning, planning your day, and always concentrating on the most valuable use of your time, can have significant consequences for your future. Making a habit of these behaviors will virtually guarantee that you will accomplish vastly more in life than the average person. Every morning, when the alarm clock goes off, you have a chance to choose once again which of these two directions you are going to go. And everything counts.

## Discipline Yourself for Success

There is one quality that, throughout the ages, has always been the critical determinant of success or failure, happiness or unhappiness, respect or disrespect, in life. And that is the quality of "self-discipline." The most successful and happy people have always been better disciplined than the least successful and the least happy.

Elbert Hubbard wrote that, "Self-discipline is the ability to make yourself do what you should do, when you should do it, whether you feel like it or not."

It is easy to do something when you feel like it, when it is fun or easy or convenient. But it is when the task is difficult and time-consuming, and you are tempted to take the line of least resistance, that discipline is required. The wonderful thing is that, the more discipline you exert on yourself, the more you like and respect yourself. You become a better and stronger person. The more discipline you practice, the more you get done and the better you feel.

Self-discipline pays off not only in terms of practical results but also in terms of a positive attitude and higher levels of self-esteem and self-regard.

## Work On Your Goals Every Day

There is perhaps no area of life where self-discipline is more important than in setting goals and working toward them every day.

In a study done by Dr. Karen Horney in New York a few years ago, participants in high school were taught goal setting. Their results were then tracked over the months and years that followed. What they learned was quite remarkable! The people in the study ended up achieving fully 95% of the goals they set in the program. Think about it! A 95%

success rate for goal setters! This is absolutely astonishing, although consistent with all we know about the subject.

They concluded scientifically what we have known throughout the centuries. All human action is purposeful. Humans set and achieve goals automatically and easily, as long as they work at them. Once you become absolutely clear about what it is you want, and then discipline yourself to do more of those things that move you toward it, your ultimate success is virtually guaranteed.

Here's the question: if goal setting and goal achieving is automatic, and built into your system, why is it that so few people have goals? The estimates, in study after study, are that only about 3% of adults have clear, written, specific goals, accompanied by plans that they work on every day. By the end of their careers, the 3% with written goals eventually earn more in financial terms than the other 97% put together.

People don't set goals for two main reasons. First, they don't realize how important goals are to a successful, happy life. Second, they don't know how to set goals. This is what we will deal with in the pages ahead.

**Seven Keys to Goal Setting**

There are seven keys to goal setting. These are general principles that apply to virtually every goal. When you find a person who is not achieving their goals, it is because of a deficiency in one of these seven key areas.

1. Write Them Down

The first key is that goals must be clear, specific, detailed and written down. A goal cannot be vague or general, like being happy or making more money. A goal must be specific, concrete, tangible and something that you can clearly visualize and imagine in your own mind.

2. Make Them Measurable

The second key to goal setting is that goals must be measurable and objective. They must be capable of being analyzed and evaluated by a third party. "Making lots of money" is not a goal. It is merely a wish or fantasy, which is common to everyone. Earning a specific amount of money within a specific period of time on the other hand, is a real goal.

3. Set Schedules and Deadlines

The third key is that goals must be time-bounded, with schedules, deadlines and sub-deadlines. In fact, there are no unrealistic goals; there are merely unrealistic deadlines. Once you have set a clear schedule and deadline for your goal, dedicate yourself to working toward achieving your goal by that time. If you don't achieve the goal by that deadline, you set another deadline, and if necessary another, and work toward that until you finally succeed.

**Goal Setting Works**

Throughout the world, many millions of people travel by air each year. Thousands of airplanes with hundreds of thousands of people crisscross the globe every day, touching down in almost every city and town. Air travel is a trillion-dollar industry that affects us all.

The success of the air travel industry, and that of every passenger, is totally the result of systematic, computerized, automatic, national goal setting. When you take a trip, you have a specific city or goal in mind. You decide exactly when you want to fly and how long it will take. You determine the distance to the airport and the time necessary to check in. You calculate how long it will take to fly to your destination, and then how long it will take to get to where you are going once you get off the plane. You set a specific schedule for every part of your journey.

Hundreds of millions of people do this every year. They successfully travel from where they are to where they want to go with incredible precision and punctuality. This is goal setting on a mass level. And the same process can work for you on a personal level.

## 4. Make Them Challenging

The fourth key to goal setting is that your goals must be challenging. They must cause you to stretch, to move out of your comfort zone. They must be beyond anything you have accomplished in the past. At the beginning, set goals with a 50% probability of success. This makes the process of striving toward the goal slightly stressful, but forcing yourself to stretch also brings out many of your best qualities.

## 5. Make Your Goals Congruent

The fifth key is that your goals must be congruent with your values and in harmony with each other. You cannot have goals that are mutually contradictory. I have met people who want to be successful in business but they want to play golf every afternoon at the same time. It is clearly not possible to realize both of these goals at the same time.

## 6. Maintain Balance

The sixth key is that your goals must be balanced, among your career or business, your financial life, your family, your health, your spiritual life and your community involvement. Just as a wheel must be balanced to revolve smoothly, your life must be balanced with goals in each area for you to be happy and fulfilled.

## 7. Set Your Major Definite Purpose

The seventh key is that you must have a major definite purpose for your life. You must have one goal, the accomplishment of which can do more to help you improve your life than any other single goal.

Your life only begins to become great when you decide upon a major definite purpose and focus all of your energies on achieving or obtaining that one single goal. Surprisingly enough, you will find yourself achieving many of your other smaller goals as you move toward achieving your major goal. But you must have a major definite purpose for your life.

In addition to the seven keys to achieving any goal, you must also have a method for goal setting and achieving that you can apply to any goal for the rest of your life.

**Goal Setting Exercise**

Here is a powerful exercise that brings everything in this chapter together into a simple process. Take out a clean sheet of paper and at the top of the page write the word "Goals," with today's date.

Then, make a list of at least ten goals that you want to accomplish in the next twelve months. Write these goals in the present tense, as though a year has passed and you have already attained the goals.

For example, if you want to weigh a certain amount, you would write, "I weigh X number of pounds by this date." If you want to earn a certain amount of money in the next twelve months, you would write, "I earn X dollars by this date."

Once you have written out your ten goals, you then review and analyze your list. You ask yourself this question, "What one goal, on this list, if I accomplished it, would have the greatest positive impact on my life?"

You read through your list of goals and select one specific goal. This goal then becomes your major definite purpose for the foreseeable future. This goal becomes your primary organizing principle. This becomes the goal that you focus on every single day.

**Begin Today**

Write your goal on a separate sheet of paper, and set a deadline.

Analyze your starting position and write out a list of reasons why you want to achieve this goal.

Identify the obstacles that stand between you and the attainment of this goal. Identify the knowledge and skills that you will need to achieve the goal. Identify the people whose cooperation and assistance you will require.

Make a plan to accomplish this goal, a series of steps organized by sequence, a checklist. You then take action on your plan and do something every day that moves you toward your major goal.

You visualize your goal as if you had already achieved it, and you resolve that you will never give up until you are successful.

Now that you have learned my world-famous goal setting process, you can now learn the success habits that will make you epically successful. There are seven habits for personal success which are true in any field, but especially if you want to earn a lot of money and become a millionaire, or even more, during your working lifetime. Since 95% of everything you do is determined by your habits, the regular practice of these behaviors can transform your life and your results.

**1. Daily Goal Setting**

As I wrote earlier, the starting point of great success is for you to develop the habit of daily goal setting. This simple habit can change your life. Many years ago, I discovered the practice of writing out my goals each day, and thinking about the things I needed to do that day to achieve them, and it transformed my life.

According to recent research, 85% or more of wealthy people have one big goal that they are working on continually. They write it down, think about it and review it all the time.

The more you program your major goal deep into your subconscious mind, the more you activate your superconscious mind, your creativity, and all of your other abilities for goal attainment.

## 2. Daily Planning

The second habit for personal success, and high productivity, is the habit of daily planning. This requires that you make a list before you begin each day. You always work from a list. According to time management experts, you can increase your productivity, performance and output by 25% to 50% the first day that you start working from a list all day long.

Once you written out a list of your activities for the day, you then set clear priorities on your tasks. You begin by organizing your list using the 80/20 Rule. What are the 20% of activities on your list that account for 80% of the value of all the items that you have to do that day?

## Use the ABCDE Method

Organize your list by using the ABCDE Method: set priorities by putting a letter next to each activity before you start work:

An A activity is something that you must do. There are serious consequences for non-performance. These are your most important tasks for the day;

A B activity is something you should do. There are mild consequences for non-completion of this task, but they are not as important as A tasks.

A C activity is something that would be nice to do, but it is not really that important. Whether you do it or not has no consequences.

A D activity is something that you delegate. The rule is to delegate everything you possibly can to free up your time to do those things that only you can do.

An E activity is something that you eliminate completely. It may be fun to do, or it may have been important in the past, but now it makes no difference at all.

The rule is that you never do a B activity when there is an A activity left undone. If you have more than one A activity, organize them by A-1, A-2, A-3, and so on.

Review your list and ask yourself this question: "If I could only do one task on this list before I was called out of town for a month, which one job would I want to be sure to get done?"

This is your A-1 task. Whatever it is, put a circle around that number and make it your top priority. Then, start to work on that task.

One of the keys to success is for you to set priorities and then live by those priorities. The road to failure is to not have priorities at all and to be constantly distracted by everything that happens in your environment.

If you can determine your top priority and start to work on that one task every morning first thing, you will double your productivity, performance and income faster than you can imagine.

3. Focus and Concentrate

The third habit of personal success is the habit of focus and concentration. These are the real keys to great wealth and achievement. Every great accomplishment has been preceded by a long period of focused concentration over an extended period of time.

Select your most important task, your top priority today, in your work, family or health, and then begin working on it first thing in the morning, before you check your email, social media or anything else.

In your work life, you select your most important task and then concentrate on it single-mindedly until it is 100% complete.

There is an important psychological discovery with regard to these success habits. If you start and complete an important task first thing each morning, you will step on the accelerator of your own potential. You will unlock your creative powers. You will kick yourself into the heightened state of "flow." You will give yourself an endorphin rush that makes you feel more powerful, more energetic, more creative, and more motivated to do even more important things.

**Task Completion**

All success is based on task completion. When you start and complete a task of any kind, it gives you a natural high, and makes you feel happy and exhilarated. If you start and complete a more important task, you will get more of a natural high. If every morning you start and complete your most important task, it actually gives you an endorphin rush that causes you to feel more powerful and confident all day long.

If you can develop the habit of starting and completing one important task each morning, you're going to become extremely successful at what you do. Your chances of becoming wealthy are going to go up like a rocket.

4. Continuous Learning

The fourth habit for personal success is the habit of continuous learning. The rule is simple: read 30 to 60 minutes each day in your field. Wealthy people read 2–3 hours each day. Keep expanding your knowledge in the most important things that you do.

Second, listen to educational audio programs in your car and on your smartphone, or when you exercise. Turn traveling time and transition time into learning time. Turn your car into a university on wheels.

Always be learning new things – even if you only listen for five or ten minutes at a time, sometimes you'll get an insight that, when added to your current knowledge, can be priceless. One new idea at the right time can be the starting point of a fortune.

Attend every seminar and workshop that you can in your field. The smartest and most experienced people in your field speak at seminars and workshops. The people who attend these seminars and workshops are usually some of the best people for you to know, meet and talk to. You can often learn more at a good convention, seminar or workshop in a few hours, or a couple of days, than you could learn on your own in months and years of study and practice.

**Always the Winners**

As a seminar leader, I find that it is always the top people who attend my seminars. It is also these same top people who come back again. The most interesting thing is when they come back months and years later and tell me their stories. Often when they came to their first seminar, they were struggling. In many cases, someone else had to pay for them to attend because they couldn't afford it.

The next time they come to a seminar, they are doing better, and the next time after that, they are doing much better. After a few years and a few seminars, plus continuous learning and hard work, they start and build their own companies. Eventually, over the years, they become rich.

Recently, two men who had come to my seminar when they were in their early 20s, just starting off in sales, came back and brought 38 members of their staff from their seven state enterprise. They said, "Your seminar made us rich."

You should be aggressive about investing in yourself and in learning new skills. As Gandhi said, "Live as though you were going to die tomorrow; but learn as if you were going to live forever."

5. Excellent Health

The fifth habit of personal success is the habit of maintaining excellent health. Watch your diet, what goes into your mouth. Resolve to eat healthy and nutritious foods, and fewer of them. Refuse to eat foods that are not really good for you.

The rule is, if you want to get to your ideal weight, it is a matter of "calories in, calories out." To lose weight, eat less and exercise more. And if you're going to eat less, eat better.

Set a goal to get 200 minutes of exercise each week, and get seven to eight hours of sleep each night.

Remember that your brain is like a battery. It gets drained over the course of the day. The more you can recharge your brain by getting lots of sleep, the more energetic and creative you will feel all day long.

6. Hard Work

The sixth reason for success is the habit of hard work. Hard work, as we said right at the very beginning of this program, is the distinguishing habit of successful people. Not just hard work, but smart work as well, work on high-value tasks.

Start an hour earlier each day. Get up by 6:00 AM and get moving. Work one hour longer each day. When everyone else goes home, stay there and get all of your work cleaned up.

Perhaps the best success principle is for you to "work all the time you work." Don't waste time. When you go to work, put your head down and work. Don't chat with your friends, drink coffee, scroll through your social accounts, read the news, or go shopping during the daytime. When you work, start off like a runner coming off the blocks at the Olympics, and just work all the time you are at work.

Imagine that they are going to do a special survey in your company to determine the hardest worker, and nobody knows about this study except you. Your job is to win the contest. Your job is to be acknowledged by everybody as the hardest worker in the company. And everyone knows who works the hardest.

Hard work will do more to bring you to the attention of people who can help you than anything else you can do in your career. And unlike many other things, how hard you work is totally under your control.

The average person today wastes fully 50% of working time, mostly in idle chitchat with co-workers and in activities that have nothing to do with the work. But not you. Instead, you make the decision that you are going to work all the time you work. When you arrive, you greet people pleasantly and then get to work. Be polite. When they ask if you have a minute to talk, you tell them, "Yes, but not right now. Right now I have to get back to work. Let's talk after work." Then, get back to work.

7. Continuous Action

Finally, the seventh success habit for personal success is the habit of continuous action. Move fast when an opportunity presents itself. Don't wait and don't delay. Make more sales calls. See more people. Study more information. Develop a fast tempo. Be quick and in motion all the time.

Most importantly, develop a sense of urgency. Only two percent of people have a sense of urgency. That two percent are known and admired by everyone around them. They accomplish more. They attract more opportunities to themselves. People will give them more jobs. They become the "go-to people" in their operations. Everyone around them knows that if you want something done quickly and well, you give it to that person.

You Will Amaze Yourself

When you begin to practice these principles in your life, you will be literally astonished at the things that you start to accomplish. You will become a more positive, powerful and effective person. You will have higher self-esteem and self-confidence. You will feel like a winner every hour of the day. You will experience a tremendous sense of personal control and direction. You will have more energy and enthusiasm. As a result, you will accomplish more in a few weeks or months than the average person might accomplish in several years.

When you become a lifelong goal setter, through study and practice, over and over again, you will program the "Master Skill of Success" into your subconscious mind. You will join the top 3% of high achievers in our society and become one of the happiest and most successful people alive.

# Vivian Weris

Vivian Weris is the CEO of a company with a great mission. Using effective neuropsychological tools and her passion, she helps women in her business leave behind their traumatic pasts and find both success and fulfillment.

She is driven by a big "why"— Vivian knows what it means to struggle through life. Growing up in a family full of violence, she ran away from home at 17 and fell into a deep depression in her early 20s. But at her lowest point, she decided to find healing. Today, she lives a happy and fulfilled life, taking the stage as a speaker, writing books, and guiding other women through her coaching and seminars, teaching them to follow her example. Vivian is driven by her desire to see her clients' lives and businesses shine .

Vivian can be reached at info@vivian-weris.de .

SCAN ME

# Chapter 2

# THE NEUROPSYCHOLOGY OF FULFILLING SUCCESS

**Vivian Weris**

## *"If we can fall, we might also spread our wings."*

Vivian Weris

Many talented entrepreneurs fail not because they lack great business ideas, but because they often stand in their own way and act for the wrong reasons. My personal story is proof of that. Despite having founded successful companies in the medical field and receiving a lot of praise, I never achieved true satisfaction because my search for success was mainly about proving myself to others.

The desire for recognition and love drove me to excel even under the most difficult circumstances. As a child of a dysfunctional family, who had run away from home at the age of 17, I started my journey to success from scratch. I was practically homeless and barely had enough money for food. But this drive to seek satisfaction through success ultimately became my downfall.

People are driven by two main motives: the search for reward and the desire to avoid pain. The expectation of reward motivates us through the release of dopamine, which drives us and provides energy and passion for our plans. This comes from a state of love. In contrast, avoiding pain causes us to act out of fear, accompanied by stress hormones such as cortisol, which cause pressure and discomfort. This response is often based on negative emotions, such as a feeling of worthlessness or fear of failure.

My desire to succeed was thus merely driven by anxiety. By trying to prove to those who had hurt me that I had value, I did not follow my personal standards of success, but rather those of the same people who had hurt me. This way, however, you will never reach your goal; someone else's definition of success simply cannot lead to your happiness and self-satisfaction.

This path inevitably involves acting against yourself and therefore hitting a wall – your own self. In my case, this cycle led to severe and debilitating depression. Every depression is experienced differently by each person, so I can only tell from my personal perspective.

When I realized that despite all efforts and success, the void inside me could never be filled, my will to live faded. I found myself in a state of emptiness and meaninglessness. Lack of purpose is a common trigger for depression, especially for action-oriented personalities like me, who primarily access the middle limbic system, where our basic emotions are located. But it wasn't just my hereditary predisposition that played a role. I was also acting against my own values and harmful beliefs clouded my perception.

It is this unique combination of actions that challenge both your hereditary predisposition and your personal values, while supporting toxic beliefs, that proves to be the ultimate secret formula for a life of unhappiness.

Now the beautiful and remarkable thing about living in this world is that everything has a flip side – if there is a formula for unhappiness, then logically there must also be a formula for happiness. This I would like to share with you in this chapter.

## The Three Pillars Principle

The path to your authenticity, which leads to success and fulfillment, is surrounded by three pillars: your genetics, your values and your beliefs. These three components form your personality. Each of these components has its own special characteristics and not all parts have the potential for change. In fact, there are parts of your personality that cannot be changed. But you can learn to deal with them in the best possible way.

## Genetics-Based Identity Mapping

It is common knowledge that traits such as body height or eye color are linked to your genes. What many people are less aware of is that a large part of our personality is also inherited. According to the latest findings in neuropsychology, the Mind Codex model identifies three personality types – the do-er, the empathizer, and the analyzer – whose behaviors are activated by different areas of the brain and thus show different needs, motives and potentials.

Interestingly, recent research suggests that differences in gender-specific characteristics are associated with cultural imprinting rather than genes. For example, the male brain can be highly empathetic, if it makes increased use of the lower limbic system, while women can be highly logical thinkers, depending on the use of their prefrontal cortex. The outdated idea that men are fundamentally more rational and women more emotional clearly is no longer up to date.

The realization that both men and women can develop each of these traits, regardless of gender and cultural environment, suggests that individuals should learn to recognize and utilize their genetic predisposition. This will help them to better understand their personal strengths and weaknesses and to achieve real success.

**Value-Based Decision-Making**

According to experts, we make approx. 20.000 decisions every day, most of them subconsciously. Although we cannot predict the outcome of these decisions for sure, we try to base them on assumptions about the future, which often leads to regret. Interestingly, we regret decisions not only because of a negative outcome, but especially when they violate our values.

Our values, embedded in the upper limbic system of the brain, can hardly be changed after the age of nine. They act as a moral compass, helping us to recognize what is right or wrong for us. The more we understand our values and their boundaries, the more confident we will become in making decisions, that we will not look back on with regret at some point.

This insight also extends to the choice of people we allow into our lives. Research shows that shared values are more important in interpersonal relationships, including marriages, than factors such as whether you want children, or finances. A relationship based on shared values is much more likely to be harmonious.

It is therefore well worth making decisions about friendships, romantic partnerships, or business relationships based on shared values. Relationships with people who do not share our values, on the other hand, can lead to constant friction. Our time and energy are precious, so we should choose wisely to whom we devote them—based on our values.

### Shaping Your External Reality Through Beliefs

The concept of "thinking, doing, having" reflects a truth that has also been proven by neuropsychology. Our beliefs shape our perception of the world through the filters we use to process information. Because of the constant influx of information, the brain has to filter, distinguishing between 'certain' and 'uncertain'. The known is classified as safe, even if it causes pain, while the unknown is classified as unsafe, even if it promises pleasure.

Our brain's priority is survival, with pain and pleasure playing a secondary role. This may explain why we often stay in toxic relationships or jobs because the brain wants to avoid leaving the 'safe' comfort zone. The brain also categorizes information into 'relevant' and 'irrelevant' based on our beliefs. So if we believe that the world is full of evil, we focus on negative events and overlook potential opportunities.

However, beliefs are changeable. With expert support, they can be transformed into positive beliefs that help us change our perceptions and thus the outcomes in our lives for the better.

## Self-confidence builds self-responsibility

Understanding the changeable parts of your personality, such as beliefs, and the unchangeable parts, such as genetics and values, is crucial to self-awareness. Self-awareness is the ability to understand yourself, and it can be learned by anyone. This ability comes with a great deal of responsibility, especially for yourself. Many avoid confronting their past and the pain associated with it, but as adults, we have a responsibility to work through that pain.

Think of responsibility as a form of power. You have the power to change situations without having to wait for permission or apologies from others. Your feelings are valid, and you can heal without an apology. Forgiveness is for your own peace, not to relativize the pain, and allows you to set boundaries without being led by anger.

Furthermore, recognizing and adjusting your beliefs and living by your values is the secret formula for happiness and success. These principles are not only applicable to your personal life, but also to business, as they help to expand your opportunities through the application of neuropsychology.

### Overcome Inner Obstacles

A lack of intelligence or a brilliant strategy is rarely the reason for failure in the start-up scene. Instead, it is often inner obstacles such as the need to please everyone, an almost compulsive desire to perform and perfectionism that cause entrepreneurs to fail. I regularly work with clients to overcome these challenges using methods from my personality training, which is based on neuropsychological insights.

**Values-Based Business Strategies:** Aligning with your values leads to more authentic and sustainable strategies.

In today's business world, where competition is fierce and markets are volatile, alignment with one's values is proving to be not only an ethical guide, but also a strategic resource. In particular, values such as harmony and peace, which are traditionally considered soft, can actually be an enormous strength. These values encourage cooperation and compromise, two factors that are essential for long-term business relationships. However, in an environment that typically rewards speed and aggressiveness, this inner focus can also be a challenge. Especially when it comes to maintaining your boundaries in negotiations and asserting yourself in the acquisition of new business.

For women in business, this challenge is multiplied. From an early age, many women are taught to avoid conflict and prioritize the needs of others—behaviors that can be misinterpreted as weakness in a business context. This upbringing subconsciously influences their decisions and actions in the business world and can be a barrier to attracting new customers. In an industry where persistence and visibility are key elements of success, women prone to this conditioning may find it more difficult to assert themselves and market their businesses effectively.

However, it is possible to turn these perceived obstacles into advantages. A values-based business strategy that recognizes and integrates these unique strengths can lead to authentic and effective leadership. Women can learn to turn their propensity for harmony and collaboration into strategic advantages by fostering a culture of inclusivity and trust, both within their teams and with their customers. By clearly defining their values and authentically incorporating them into their business strategies, they can achieve a strong market positioning and ultimately pave the way for long-term success.

**Transforming Belief Systems:** Transforming limiting beliefs helps entrepreneurs successfully overcome challenges.

Transforming belief systems is an essential step for entrepreneurs on the path to authentic success and personal liberation. Deep-rooted beliefs, such as the assumption that our sense of security and worth depends on the satisfaction or success of others, can be inhibiting and lead to destructive patterns such as people-pleasing and excessive pressure to perform. These beliefs, often formed in childhood, serve as invisible chains that prevent you from reaching your full potential. When you realize that such beliefs are malleable, you open up the possibility of freeing yourself from them and embracing a healthier way of thinking and acting.

Many of us harbor the belief that the only way to prove our worth is through success. This belief can lead to a never-ending cycle of pressure to perform, leaving you exhausted and demotivated in the long run. If you learn to re-evaluate success—not as external recognition or material gain, but as fulfillment and authenticity in line with your deepest values—then you can create an environment where true satisfaction and sustainable success are possible.

Perfectionism is another obstructive belief system that traps you in the illusion that mistakes are unacceptable and that everything you do must be flawless. This belief inevitably leads to procrastination and paralysis because it is ultimately impossible to achieve perfection. Working on this belief, recognizing that mistakes are part of the learning and growth process, allows you to let go of the 'perfect' moment and take bold steps forward. It also opens up a world where small steps of progress and continuous improvement are celebrated (rather than a distant, unattainable goal), which enhances both your personal and professional development.

Actively working on your belief systems and transforming them a little more each day, opens the door to unprecedented levels of freedom, effectiveness, and satisfaction in both your professional and personal lives. It is a journey that requires courage and perseverance, but the fruits of this labor are undoubtedly worth it.

**Self-Responsibility And Business Management:** Taking personal responsibility for managing yourself and your business is crucial to efficiency and success.

In a dynamic business world with all its uncertainties, personal responsibility is much more than an empty buzzword; it is the very foundation of successful business management. It applies to our personal leadership as well as to the management of our company. The ability to go beyond our own limits and free ourselves from limiting behavioral patterns such as the constant need for recognition, excessive pressure to perform, or the pursuit of perfection is a crucial leadership skill. It is not just about our individual way of working, but about the entire working atmosphere, the corporate culture, and, ultimately, the success of our company.

For successful leaders, creating an inspiring work environment that encourages—and even requires—individual responsibility and initiative is paramount. Such an environment enables each team member to contribute fully, while developing a sense of satisfaction and appreciation. For women in leadership positions in particular, overcoming traditional role patterns, such as avoiding conflict, offers a unique opportunity to redefine corporate culture. This creates a working environment that promotes diversity, equality, and the appreciation of each individual team member as an integral part of the team.

To summarize, the true essence of empowerment and leadership is to seize the opportunity to see and actively shape your organization and your professional role within it as a reflection of your personality. If you can transform your personal beliefs and integrate your values into your daily business life, you will lay the foundation for both your personal success and the success of our company. Only by acting and leading authentically will you strengthen your team and your business internally, as well as the external perception of your business and yourself by customers, employees, and business partners alike.

## Your Next Level – My Offer To You

Surely, you have recognized yourself in at least one of these patterns. I want to make it clear at this point that you are never trapped in your inner blocks and pain. You can always choose to take responsibility and therefore control.

Your business needs a strong foundation, and your authenticity in particular is essential to achieving both success and fulfillment. With your authentic strength, you can take on the challenges of entrepreneurship and attract the people who are right for you and your business. Entrepreneurship can be fun; it can feel easy. And it will be if you use simple neuropsychological methods to understand your brain structure and psyche, and learn successful transformation processes.

I would like to give you the chance to unlock your full potential by offering you a free consultation. During this session, we will design a personalized strategy plan to help you achieve your goals and finally attract joy, success, and fulfillment into your life—not magically, but scientifically.

Contact us today to secure one of our limited free appointments.

# Medhat Zaki

Medhat Zaki is a dynamic Egyptian-German entrepreneur, author, and investor who has made a name for himself in the world of business growth and marketing consultancy. Having migrated to Germany in 2001, he focused on studying business and honed his skills as an international sales manager, selling products across several countries. He then moved on to become a sales trainer, expanding his scope by studying negotiation tactics, business models, and planning, and the psychology of the super-rich, which he believes is the key to achieving financial freedom.

Today, Medhat is a highly sought-after consultant, helping businesses in Germany and the Middle East to develop winning strategies, boost their sales, and grow their revenue. His expertise in business modeling and planning, coupled with his vast experience in sales and marketing, makes him the go-to consultant for businesses looking to scale and achieve their goals. With his contagious energy and passion for business, Medhat is undoubtedly a force to reckon with in the world of entrepreneurship.

SCAN ME

# Chapter 3

# RISE ABOVE THE SEA OF SAMENESS

**Medhat Zaki**

## "Always Strive to Get On Top in Life Because It's The Bottom That's Overcrowded."
Les Brown

When marketing feels like noise and consumers seem immune, is there any point in trying? The answer is a resounding yes – but success demands a clear understanding of both the challenges and the transformative power of branding and positioning. Done poorly, marketing contributes to the cacophony that consumers tune out. But executed strategically, marketing is the vital tool that elevates a product or service, creating an identity that resonates with its intended audience and fosters genuine connection. And there's more; in a world of overwhelming choice, familiarity breeds confidence. This is where branding shines, offering consumers a safe harbor amidst the storm of messages.

### The Mere Exposure Effect: Familiarity Breeds Confidence

In consumer psychology, there's a powerful phenomenon at play that often goes unnoticed: the mere exposure effect. This principle states that the more familiar we are with something, the more likely we are to develop a preference for it. It's a subconscious process that influences our decisions and behaviors in countless ways, from the products we buy to the people we trust.

At its core, familiarity provides a sense of security and comfort. As humans, we're naturally drawn to things that we recognize and understand. This is why, when faced with a choice between a brand we know and a new, untested option, most of us will instinctively reach for the familiar.

Let's consider a common scenario: shopping for a new pair of shoes. You find yourself torn between two options – a stylish pair from a brand you've never heard of and a classic design from a well-known brand you've worn before. Even if the unfamiliar pair catches your eye, there's a good chance you'll end up choosing the trusted brand. Why? Because you know what to expect. You've experienced the fit, the quality, and the comfort of that brand before, and that familiarity gives you confidence in your decision.

The mere exposure effect is even more pronounced in situations where the stakes are higher. When traveling abroad, for example, many people seek out familiar fast food chains like McDonald's or Burger King, and not necessarily for the taste or the nutritional value. No, it's because in an unfamiliar environment, these brands offer a comforting sense of consistency and reliability.

> ***"It is your ability to deliver on the promise that determines your brand for the future"***
> Brian Tracy

As a marketer or business owner, understanding the mere exposure effect is crucial to building a strong brand. By consistently delivering on your promises and maintaining a cohesive brand identity across all touchpoints, you can cultivate a sense of familiarity and trust with your audience. The more people see and interact with your brand in a positive way, the more likely they are to choose you over the competition.

Of course, familiarity alone isn't enough to guarantee success. Your product or service still needs to deliver value and meet the needs of your target market. But by leveraging the power of the mere exposure effect, you can create a strong foundation of trust and loyalty that will serve your brand for years to come.

But like in any journey in life, defining where you want to go is not enough. You'll also need a strong idea of the landscape through which you'll travel. In marketing, this aspect is called positioning.

## The Water Bottle Analogy: The Importance of Positioning

Imagine you're walking through a supermarket, and you spot a bottle of water priced at just 50 cents. It's a bargain, and you don't think twice about adding it to your cart. Now, picture yourself at the airport, about to board a flight. That same bottle of water suddenly costs $3 or more. And if you find yourself on a plane, the price skyrockets even further. But the most extreme example? Imagine you're on an adventure in the middle of a desert, desperate for hydration. At that moment, you'd be willing to pay almost anything for a single bottle of water. And, what's more, you probably aren't even concerned about the brand at all anymore.

This simple analogy illustrates the profound impact of positioning on perceived value. The water itself doesn't change, but the context in which it's offered can dramatically alter its worth in the eyes of the consumer. The same principle applies to your brand and your products or services.

Too often, businesses make the mistake of investing heavily in branding without giving equal consideration to positioning. They pour resources into creating a stunning logo, designing eye-catching packaging, and developing a clever tagline – but they neglect to think strategically about where and how they're presenting their brand to the world. As a result, they find themselves struggling to gain traction and wondering why their marketing efforts aren't yielding the desired results.

*"Bad positioning is like throwing money out the window of a skyscraper. Only If you're lucky, the wind might blow some of it back to you, but most of it will be gone"*
Medhat Zaki

But positioning goes beyond just physical location or distribution channels. It's also about the promises you make and, more importantly, the promises you keep. Consistency is key when it comes to building trust and credibility with your audience. If your brand is positioned as a luxury option, for example, every touchpoint needs to reinforce that premium experience. If you promise exceptional customer service, you need to deliver on that promise every single time.

This is where fast food chains like McDonald's and Burger King excel. They've positioned themselves as reliable, convenient options that offer a consistent experience, regardless of where in the world you encounter them. Whether you're in New York, Tokyo, or Sydney, you know exactly what to expect when you walk into one of these restaurants. They've made a promise to their customers, and they work tirelessly to keep that promise with every interaction.

> *"Positioning is finding the right parking space inside the consumer's mind and going for it before someone else takes it"*
> Laura Busche, author and branding expert

Now, as you develop your own brand positioning strategy, ask yourself: What promises am I making to my audience? How can I consistently deliver on those promises across every touchpoint? Where and how should I be presenting my brand to maximize its perceived value and resonance with my target market? What can I do to earn that parking space inside my dream clients' heads?

By answering these questions and aligning your branding efforts with a strong positioning strategy, you'll be well on your way to building an authentic, memorable brand that stands out in a crowded marketplace. But the journey doesn't end there.

**From Product Branding to Personal Branding**

In the past few years, branding has evolved far beyond the realm of products and services in our ever more digitally connected world. Increasingly, individuals recognize the power and necessity of cultivating a strong personal brand. Whether you're an entrepreneur, a freelancer, or a professional climbing the corporate ladder, your personal brand is a crucial asset that can open doors, build trust, and set you apart from the crowd.

> *"If you don't give the market the story to talk about, they'll define your brand's story for you."*
> David Brier, branding and brand identity expert and author of Brand Intervention

At its core, personal branding is about taking control of your own narrative and shaping the way others perceive you. To achieve that, you need to understand your unique strengths, values, and expertise, and communicate them in a consistent, authentic way across all channels. Just as a well-crafted product brand can evoke specific emotions and associations in the minds of consumers, a strong personal brand can influence how people feel about you and what they believe you're capable of achieving.

Consumers are increasingly drawn to the human element behind the brands they interact with. They want to know the stories, the faces, and the values that drive the companies they support.

Personal branding also influences consumer impressions and decisions. People tend to prefer the product or service with a strong, relatable personal brand. They'll choose the coach who empowers clients to achieve their goals, or the consultant who creatively solves challenging problems. Statistics support this approach. In a recent study by a major retailer, over 70 percent of customers research products – and suppliers – extensively before making the transaction. And with a strong personal brand, you can stand out in a sea of sameness.

Now, a great personal brand requires more than a fancy logo or a big social media presence. I've found that true, effective branding requires the implementation of five core concepts across all elements of your career.

**1. Specialization:** Trying to be a jack-of-all-trades will only dilute your brand and confuse your audience. Instead, identify the one thing you do better than anyone else and make that the cornerstone of your brand.

**2. Be a leader in your field:** To build a strong brand, you need to position yourself as a leader in your industry. This doesn't necessarily mean you have to be in a formal leadership role; it's about being recognized as an expert, an innovator, and a thought leader.

**3. Your brand should be an authentic reflection of who you are as a person.** It should align with your values, your passions, and your unique personality traits. Don't try to be someone you're not or mimic the branding of others. Instead, embrace what makes you different and infuse your brand with your own personal style and flair.

**4. Dare to be different:** You need to find ways to stand out and be memorable. Search for opportunities to put a unique spin on your brand—don't be afraid to take risks and think outside the box. The more distinctive and recognizable your brand is, the more likely it is to stick in people's minds.

**5. ... but tell a consistent story:** Your visual identity, your messaging, your actions, and your values should all tell the same story and reinforce the same brand promise. Consistency is key when it comes to building trust and credibility with your audience.

It might sound simple, and it actually is. The one thing that differentiates successful (personal) brands from those struggling, is consistency and effort over a long period of time. The above-mentioned principles are not a one-off thing. The art of successful branding is more a marathon than a sprint. It's about what you do, time and time again – but also who you do it with.

## The Power of Association: Leveraging the Influence of Others

You might have heard the old adage, "you are the company you keep". The people and brands you associate with can have a profound impact on how others perceive you and your own brand. This is known as the power of association, and it's a critical factor to consider as you build and grow your personal brand.

Think of it like this: when you see someone constantly spending time with successful, influential people in your industry, you naturally assume that they must be successful and influential as well. On the flip side, if you see someone hanging around with people who have a negative reputation or are known for unethical behavior, that association can tarnish their own brand by proxy.

The power of association works on a psychological level. As humans, we're wired to make snap judgments and categorize people based on the limited information we have about them. When we see someone associating with people or brands we admire and respect, we subconsciously transfer those positive feelings to that person as well. It's a shortcut our brains use to help us make sense of the world and decide who we should trust and pay attention to.

But the power of association doesn't just apply to formal partnerships or collaborations. It's also about the more subtle ways you position yourself and your brand in relation to others. The events you attend, the content you share on social media, the people you interact with in your blog posts or podcasts—all of these choices send signals about who you are, what you value, and where you fit into your industry's ecosystem.

One way to think about it is the concept of "borrowed sunshine." Just as a planet or moon can bask in the glow of a nearby star, you can benefit from the "glow" of someone else's well-established brand. But it's important to remember that borrowed sunshine is just that—borrowed. To truly build a strong, lasting brand, you need to cultivate your own sources of light and heat. The goal is not to ride on someone else's coattails indefinitely, but rather to use those strategic associations as a launchpad for your brand's growth and success.

**Speaking From Experience**

As an author and a coach, I've had the privilege of guiding countless individuals and businesses on their branding journeys. But my own path to success was far from a straight line. In fact, it was a series of twists, turns, and hard-earned lessons that ultimately led me to where I am now.

Growing up in Egypt, I struggled academically and chose to forgo a traditional university education in favor of starting my own business. At first, I found success through hard work and determination, even hiring a team of employees to support my growing venture. But I lacked a clear vision and strategy for the long term. I was working hard, but I wasn't working smart.

Then, tragedy struck. A series of terrorist attacks targeting tourists in Egypt decimated my business, which relied heavily on hotel bookings. Overnight, I lost everything. I had to let go of my staff, shut down my operations, and start from scratch in a new country.

It was a long and rocky road, but today, I have the privilege of working closely with Brian and other influential figures in my industry. We've co-authored books, shared stages, and collaborated on countless projects. And I can say without hesitation that these relationships have been instrumental in my success.

But here's the thing: my journey is not unique. The power of association and collaboration is available to anyone who's willing to put in the work and stay true to their authentic personal brand. You don't need to have a famous mentor or a massive following to benefit from the influence of others. You just need to be strategic, consistent, and genuine in your approach.

As you build your own personal brand, remember that success is not a solo endeavor. Seek out opportunities to learn from and collaborate with others in your industry. Attend conferences and events, join online communities, and don't be afraid to reach out to people you admire. You never know where a single connection might lead.

And most importantly, stay true to yourself. Your personal brand is a reflection of who you are and what you stand for. Don't try to be someone you're not, or chase after trends that don't align with your values. The most successful personal brands are the ones that are authentic, consistent, and infused with personality.

If I had to pick out one takeaway for you from this chapter as being the most important one, it is this: your personal brand is a critical asset that can make the difference between blending in and standing out, between struggling to find clients and having them seek you out, between feeling stuck and unfulfilled and building a thriving, impactful business that aligns with your values and goals.

Yes, building a strong personal brand takes time, effort, and consistency. But here's the good news: you don't have to go it alone. In fact, one of the most powerful ways to accelerate your personal branding journey is to collaborate with and learn from others who have already achieved what you aspire to.

## My Offer to You

That's where I come in. As an author, coach, and collaborator, I've had the privilege of working with some of the most influential figures in the business world, including my own mentor and friend, Brian Tracy. And I've seen firsthand the incredible impact that these collaborations can have on one's personal brand and success.

Imagine the credibility and exposure you could gain by being featured in a book alongside Brian Tracy and other industry leaders. Picture the doors that could open and the relationships you could build by joining a curated community of high-achieving entrepreneurs. And think about the impact you could make by sharing your message and expertise with a wider audience, all while staying true to your authentic personal brand.

If this sounds like the kind of support and acceleration you're looking for, I invite you to take the first step today. Reach out to me directly to learn more about the collaboration and coaching opportunities available. Let's have a conversation about your goals, your challenges, and how I can help you achieve the success and impact you deserve.

# Jordan Myers

Jordan Myers is an accomplished business professional who has previously worked as a Licensed Stock Broker and is now a Licensed Real Estate Broker. He is also the owner of three successful companies, surpassing $150 Million. Jordan's primary focus in life is being a dedicated husband and father, and he actively contributes to his community through various philanthropic endeavors. He believes that succeeding in business, or anything in life, begins with setting the mind to achieve a certain level of success. The outcome is directly related to the effort an individual puts into their endeavors, without any doubt that success will be achieved, regardless of external factors. In recognition of his outstanding contributions, Jordan was honored with the Palm Harbor, Florida Citizen of the Year award. Additionally, Jordan has served on the Board of Directors for multiple organizations and lives by the motto "Outwork 'em!"

# Chapter 4

# OUTWORK 'EM

**Jordan Myers**

I was always told by my father to "outwork 'em." He would repeat this phrase daily, whether it pertained to playing sports, schoolwork, studying for a test, or working on a group project. It didn't matter what goal or aspiration I mentioned; his response was always the same. The level of work required depends on the level of achievement one seeks. While it is possible to achieve more by working longer hours, studying more, or elevating your skills, putting in more hours does not always guarantee success over the competition.

Have you ever looked at someone and thought, "Wow, they are so talented. How do they make it look so effortless?" or "They are just a natural." Why do some things seem to come easily to others when they are so difficult for us? We all live two different lives: one when we are around others and one when we are alone. The way people perceive us and what they know about us is based on how we interact and present ourselves in front of them. However, what people don't truly understand is what we do when no one is watching. When we wonder how something is so easy for someone else, we don't know if it came naturally to them or if they had to work hard to achieve it. They may have dedicated countless hours to improving their knowledge and skills to reach where they are now. What we see is the end result, and we judge them based on that, often comparing ourselves to their achievements. When we witness someone performing well, it may seem like they are just naturally gifted, and it came easily to them. However, we don't truly know the effort and sacrifices they made to reach that level of performance.

We all have a natural level of talent that varies depending on the task at hand. For instance, consider a professional basketball player. They may have a physique that is better suited to playing basketball than most people reading this. However, this does not necessarily mean that they, or any other person of similar size, will automatically play basketball at a high level. Nor does it mean that someone of smaller size would never be able to compete against them. The ability to compete at the same level is possible. Anything less than this is a limitation that exists only in the mind.

Now, let's examine the top performers in your industry. Are their production levels attainable for you? Absolutely. How do you compare to them? Is your production lower, equal to, or higher than your competition? Understanding how you measure up against your competition will provide you with a reference point and help guide your improvement efforts. Otherwise, you won't know if you're performing at your best or if there's room for improvement. When setting goals for our businesses, it's crucial to be aware of the production levels we can currently achieve and those that represent the highest attainable ability. This way, we can better identify the skills and knowledge we need to enhance in order to maximize productivity. Without these benchmarks and a stretch goal, we often find ourselves drifting aimlessly.

Have you ever been told, "You can do anything you set your mind to?" Setting the mind could involve determining a specific goal, intention, or priority. It's about defining what you want to achieve and aligning your thoughts, actions, and behaviors to work towards those objectives. This can contribute to a sense of purpose and direction in one's life. Individuals who intentionally direct their attention to the present moment, clear their minds of distractions, calm their thoughts, and cultivate a sense of awareness are setting their minds in this sense. This can lead to improved concentration, resulting in intense focus on their goals.

Now, once it has been determined what needs to be done, it is time to start working. Your success will be directly determined by the effort you put into the task. We frequently hear the phrase "hard work," which may imply that it is not easy or that the more difficult the task, the less likely it is to be achievable. However, the goal is attainable; it simply requires intense focus and discipline, which can be the most challenging aspects. For example, throwing a dart at a bull's eye is not physically demanding. You stand still and only move your arm at the elbow. So why do average people struggle to consistently hit the bull's eye? It is not because throwing a dart weighing 18–26 grams is physically hard work. If you miss the bull's eye, is it the target's fault? The game, like most tasks in life, is 90% mental. Visualizing a target, practicing and perfecting the skills necessary to perform the task, and being able to consistently give maximum effort lead to successful results.

Whatever you are seeking to achieve, look to your competition and use their presence as motivation to surpass them. If your competition is not performing at a high level, it may not require all your willpower to outperform them. However, if the person you are aiming to outwork is performing at the highest level, it will take immense strength and commitment to outdo them, demanding peak effort from an individual.

Only you know how much effort you put into a certain task. It is possible for almost anyone to lose 10 pounds (4.54 kg) in one day, with true 100% effort in cutting the weight. Think of the day in your business or schooling where you gave the most effort. Was that all of your effort, or could you have done even a little more? Many times, we confuse success with giving maximum effort, but we can succeed without giving maximum effort. However, we will never reach our full potential without giving maximum effort. Effort is the key that unlocks potential. Our bodies may not be able to go 100% at all times, which is why it is important to take care of our health, mind, and body. When we must be on for our business, we can give maximum effort. This way, we can have a good work-life balance. When we give minimal effort at work, we tend to bring the work home or think about the work we didn't do during the day, instead of being present with our life outside of work. If we give maximum effort at work, our likelihood of success significantly increases, and then we are fully comfortable completing our workday and moving on to our life outside of work. What would your results look like if you gave 100% of your willpower for just one day?

How do you track effort? Often, effort is more easily trackable with physical labor. If two people are doing the same task, but one has a significantly higher output, it could likely be attributed to the greater effort put in by that person. Now, if you are in a sales position that involves making phone calls or setting appointments, imagine a day when you made the highest number of calls ever recorded in the history of your profession. Make one goal after reading this book. Tomorrow, make an unwavering promise to yourself to exert the utmost effort in your business. Release any fear, concerns about market conditions, or anything beyond your control. While thinking is crucial for planning, when it's time to take action, don't hesitate, just do it.

There are tasks that may seem unachievable or too difficult, such as losing fifty pounds, or running a marathon in the next year. However, it's important to remember that these goals are achievable, but they present a challenge that you haven't mastered yet. Before becoming frustrated, think about your greatest accomplishment in life. Was it something you were interested in or enjoyed doing? Reflect on the work, dedication, and mindset you had while achieving that task. Did it come easily, or was there a point where it became easier after all the hard work and sacrifice? Think about the progress you made along the way, both in your successes and failures. Document your strengths and weaknesses and find ways to improve your performance.

Vision is often considered the greatest of our five senses. However, its limitation is that what we see regularly becomes our reality because it is right in front of us and finite. As a result, we tend to live from an outside-in perspective, letting our environment and surroundings control our conscious minds. Our minds are infinite, and if we live inside-out, we take control of our thoughts, attitude, and response to every moment of our lives. In business, we tend to focus on daily numbers and results, neglecting our daily mindset and how certain things can be implanted into our minds, making them appear real when they are actually science fiction and could never happen. Fear, worry, and doubt frequently control our ability to take action, and we make up stories to justify our inaction. These stories are often made up and do not exist in reality. Our minds have the ability to perceive things as reality, but they are typically just perceptions and not reality at all. We can control our minds and thoughts at all times, but most people are susceptible to allowing exterior influences to control their thoughts. This is living from an outside-in perspective.

Living inside-out can be our biggest challenge every day. The more we focus on our mindset, getting and maintaining it to peak performance, the better. Peak performance refers to a state of optimal functioning and excellence in performance. It is the ability to consistently perform at one's best and achieve exceptional results in a specific area or endeavor. Whether in sports, academics, professional work, or any other domain, peak performance involves reaching and maintaining a high level of performance consistently.

Have you ever heard of an athlete being "in the zone"? Everything seems to go right for them; their skills appear to be at peak performance, and they can't miss. Being in the zone is when one experiences a state of flow, which is a mental state characterized by complete immersion and focus in an activity. It's a state of optimal performance where time seems to fly by, and you're fully absorbed in what you're doing. A flow state, also known as being "in the zone," refers to a mental state of optimal performance and deep immersion in an activity. It was first described by positive psychologist Mihaly Csikszentmihalyi. In this state, individuals experience a heightened sense of focus, concentration, and enjoyment while engaging in a task.

When in a state of flow, people often lose track of time and feel completely absorbed in what they are doing. They are fully engaged and highly productive, experiencing a sense of effortless control over their actions. The activity itself becomes intrinsically rewarding, and individuals may describe feeling joy, creativity, and success.

Entering a state of flow does not happen by chance. The science behind being in the zone is a combination of precise decision-making and sustained attention to detail. When in a flow state, the worry typically felt before a task is now nonexistent, and the experience becomes autotelic.

Now, if you are already outperforming everyone, you become the benchmark. Your competition is looking at you, and the best are giving their maximum effort to surpass your performance. Only you truly know the commitment and effort required to reach the level you are performing at, which now becomes the level that you must exceed, more than others who are using your past performance as a gauge to outdo you.

It is important to note that hard work is not synonymous with overworking or burning out. It is about working smartly and efficiently, maintaining a healthy work-life balance, and recognizing the value of rest and self-care in sustaining long-term effort. To outwork someone means to surpass their effort and productivity levels. If you are looking to outwork someone, here are some strategies you can consider:

**1. Set clear goals:** Define specific and achievable goals for yourself. Break them down into actionable steps and prioritize them based on importance and urgency. Having clear goals helps you stay focused and motivated.

**2. Develop a strong work ethic:** cultivate a strong work ethic characterized by dedication, discipline, and a commitment to excellence. Be willing to put in the time and effort required to accomplish your tasks and goals.

**3. Improve time management:** enhance your time management skills to maximize your productivity. Identify your most productive hours and schedule your most important and challenging tasks during that time. Minimize distractions and prioritize your workload effectively.

**4. Embrace a growth mindset:** adopt a growth mindset that views challenges and failures as opportunities for learning and growth. Embrace a positive attitude towards setbacks and use them as motivation to work harder and improve.

**5. Focus on productivity, not just busy-ness.** It is essential to distinguish between being busy and being productive. Focus on meaningful and high-impact tasks that move you closer to your goals, rather than simply staying busy. Prioritize tasks that have the most significant impact on your success.

**6. Continuous improvement:** seek opportunities for continuous learning and improvement. Stay updated on industry trends, invest in professional development, and acquire new skills that give you a competitive edge. Aim to continually enhance your knowledge and expertise.

**7. Maintain discipline and consistency:** consistency is key when it comes to outworking someone. Maintain a disciplined routine and consistently show up to work on your goals, even when motivation may wane. Develop habits that support your productivity and avoid procrastination.

**8. Develop efficiency and effectiveness:** look for ways to work more efficiently and effectively. Streamline processes, automate tasks where possible, and seek out tools or techniques that can help you work smarter, not just harder.

**9. Seek feedback and learn from others:** be open to feedback and learn from those who excel in their field. Surround yourself with high-performers or mentors who can provide guidance and insights. Take their advice and implement strategies that have been proven to be effective.

**10. Take care of yourself:** to consistently outwork someone, it is important to prioritize self-care. Ensure you get sufficient rest, engage in regular exercise, and maintain a healthy work-life balance. Taking care of your well-being enhances your focus, productivity, and overall performance.

Remember, the goal is not solely to outwork someone for the sake of competition, but to achieve your personal and professional growth. Focus on your own progress and improvement, and let your dedication and effort speak for themselves.

When hard work is purposeful and balanced, it can lead to personal growth, success, and achieving one's aspirations. In his book "Think and Grow Rich", Napoleon Hill emphasizes the importance of focusing on wealth abundance. To simplify, find a task you're passionate about, excel at it, and give your all. This will lead to success and financial stability, as your high-quality work will outpace the competition in any market.

# Maria Solodar

Maria Solodar is a social media expert and author of a unique grow-and-monetize content strategy for Instagram. She attracted over four million subscribers without paid advertising, dancing, or jokes — solely on expert content, and made sales in the eight-figure range to this audience. Over 2,000,000 people have completed her programs on online sales, and she has developed her own method for building an audience and making sales on social media for authors, experts, and entrepreneurs.

By using these technologies, you can attract free followers, build a large audience based on your authenticity and expertise, and make them want your product without being salesy. Read this chapter to learn more about this method, and visit Solodar.com for more materials, guides, and ready-made templates for your social media.

# Chapter 5

# THE SECRET SYSTEM OF EXPERT CONTENT ON INSTAGRAM THAT BROUGHT ME EIGHT-FIGURE SUMS.

**Maria Solodar**

Your card has been declined.

With a dismissive look, the Heathrow Airport employee took the biscuits and tea from the counter that I had spent the previous twenty minutes trying to pay for, and walked away, giving me a chance to withdraw in silence. None of my cards worked.

Just two weeks earlier, I had been a successful entrepreneur, a millionaire, flying in private jets, travelling in a Rolls-Royce with a private chauffeur, earning so much for so many years that I had forgotten the feeling of not being able to buy what I wanted. And yet, the ten-euro purchase of tea and biscuits turned out to be out of reach.

But the fact that I didn't have a penny didn't bother me at that moment. Nor did I have the resources to think that all my cards and accounts would be blocked, that the businesses I had built up over ten years would cease to exist, that my husband stopped speaking to me and I understood that it was forever. None of this compared to the main problem: there was a war in my country. My parents were in a danger zone where bombs fell every minute, news of destroyed houses in my street, the death of acquaintances… My sister was due to give birth these days, and all I saw were headlines about rockets being fired at maternity hospitals.

Without above-mentioned tea, I walked to the jetway, my brain in a fog. And twelve hours later, I stepped out of Los Angeles airport with my eyes squinting. A new life was beginning in a big, unknown country, and I had no idea what it would be like. There was no foothold. After all, I, a citizen of Ukraine, where the war had started a few days earlier, was running an international business in all the countries of Eastern Europe, and the headquarters of my company, along with all its assets, were in Moscow.

I decided to close the business and leave in one day, thus losing all sources of income. International banks blocked

Russian accounts, Russia denied Ukrainian citizens trans-actions with assets and withdrawal of funds abroad. So all my assets, everything I had created and earned over the last ten years, were alienated. My then husband had the opposite political stance; it turned out that we had entire-ly different values and our marriage was destroyed, it was time to separate. On this scorched earth of my formerly successful life, I was forced to move to the USA.

It's easy for me to write about that terrible time now — sitting in a cozy café on the first floor of my building in Manhattan. My new business in the US is thriving, I have a green card for talented people and all the documentation, I am invited to red carpets, my clients include world celebrities. The contrast between these two women is colossal, it's not just two years, it's a massive divide. And Instagram saved my life, in every sense of the word, and became the reason for all the positive changes I have listed. How? — you might ask.

This is what this chapter is about.

**Be True to Yourself**

Growing up in a modest two-street neighborhood, shar-ing a single bathroom and toilet with dozens of families, my early life was far from affluent. Our food came straight from the garden, and instead of playing with my peers, I immersed myself in books, dreaming of travelling, meet-ing fascinating people and achieving fame. These aspira-tions seemed unattainable in our social reality, where in-ternational travel was unheard of, and my ambitions were met with skepticism.

Everything changed with the introduction of the Internet in our home. It opened up a world where I could communi-cate with anyone in the world and explore beautiful places through video. More importantly, it gave me a platform to express myself freely and anonymously. As an introverted and often ridiculed child, the online world allowed me to share my thoughts and experiences without fear of judgement. I started with a blog and progressed from local networks to platforms like Live Journal, where I wrote down my dreams, reflections, and emotions.

But the advent of the internet not only gave me a voice, it connected me to like-minded people around the world. Discovering that others shared my experiences and feelings was empowering. As I wrote and shared more openly, my circle of virtual friends grew into the hundreds, and with the rise of social networking sites by the end of high school, my followers numbered in the thousands. This trend continued into university, where I graduated with a significant online following, all because I remained authentic.

## Authenticity Translates Into Profit

This authenticity has enabled me to travel to over 100 countries, publish a bestselling book and significantly improve my family's living conditions, including buying an apartment for my mother — our family's first home. I broke new ground in my family by becoming the first entrepreneur and millionaire. Even after losing everything and having to start over in a new country with a different language and culture, I've proved that it's possible to achieve your dreams and earn a substantial income through social media, just by being true to yourself.

Contrary to popular belief, success on social media doesn't depend on having exceptional dancing skills, a charismatic personality, model looks or celebrity status. Most successful bloggers are just ordinary people sharing their passions, whether it's fashion, moving abroad, fishing, cooking, cars, relationships, or parenting. It's their authenticity and passion that attracts people, not perfection. Any kind of content has an audience among the billions of people online, as long as it's created with sincerity.

## My Three Pillars of Success

**1.Authority and expertise** are critical to success in the digital space. My personal journey of sharing professional experiences, challenges, and successes helped position me as an expert in my field. This credibility encouraged customers to contact me directly, bypassing the need for explicit calls to action.

Many attribute poor sales to small audiences, but the real determinant is the demonstration of expertise. In one case, I helped a humor blogger with eleven million followers and a market expert with just 300 followers. Despite similar strategies, the expert generated over $1,000,000 in sales, significantly outperforming the humor blogger's $100,000. The difference? The humor blogger's audience, accustomed to entertainment, did not see him as an authoritative figure or trust him as a credible source for purchases.

**2.Create a desire** in the client to change their life. My followers witnessed first-hand my journey from financial hardship and tedious jobs to success through internet marketing. My life transformation demonstrated the potential of what they could achieve. Many of my subscribers weren't initially familiar with internet marketing or how to use social networks to generate income, but they were drawn to the possibilities because they saw the tangible changes in my life.

However, simply presenting a product is often not enough to effectively engage an audience. Most people may not recognize their dissatisfaction with their current circumstances as a solvable problem. They may endure rather than seek solutions. This is where powerful content comes in, inspiring and illustrating a vision of what could be so that they want the same changes for themselves.

**3.Product.** As I said — the most attractive and interesting content is created with passion. I'm the kind of person who can't force myself to do boring things. I loved what I was doing, and I generously shared stories about my work with the world. This approach gave my audience a dynamic and authentic view of my professional life, far more engaging than any website description or sales pitch could ever be. As a result, my services were always in high demand, negating the need for direct sales tactics.

## How To Foster Genuine Interest

I learned the true potential of my social network management approach from an unexpected success: making my first million in less than a day. When a leading national blogger, admired by many, approached me to apply my strategies to her blog, the results were staggering. Our launch attracted tens of thousands of people, overwhelming technical platforms with the sheer volume of traffic. This success story spread quickly, attracting the interest of celebrities from all walks of life, eager to replicate our success. For over a decade, I've applied these principles to numerous campaigns, proving their effectiveness across the board.

Despite Instagram's huge sales potential, many struggle to achieve significant results. The common mistake is to produce content that focuses solely on audience consumption, without engaging them in any meaningful way. When it's time to sell, authors often introduce direct advertising, which leads to decreased engagement due to the promotional nature of these posts. People use social media primarily for entertainment and quality content, not to be sold to, which is why direct advertising tends to fail.

Unlike direct advertising's call to action, my approach involves storytelling and engagement that gradually "warms up" the audience. Warming up is a strategic process of developing your relationship with your audience from mere acquaintances to loyal fans who are excited about buying your products. In sales terminology, prospects who are unfamiliar with your product are referred to as "cold" leads, as opposed to "hot" leads who are already inclined to buy. Although only a minority of prospects are ready to buy, the majority are cold and need to be nurtured.

This nurturing process effectively warms up the audience, making them more receptive and eager to purchase your offering, even before details such as price or availability are revealed. Imagine creating such anticipation for your products that your audience actively and enthusiastically seeks out purchases, eliminating the need for overt sales tactics.

In reality, whether spoken by a sales manager on the phone, written in an email or on a landing page, selling involves the same conceptual elements:

- **Actualization** and selling the topic — explain what its essence is, making the audience understand that there is a way out of complex, painful situations.

- **"Your transformation story"** — tell your story, comparing "before" and "after"

- **Debunking myths** — gather misconceptions that put potential buyers off and debunk them in your storytelling before you even start selling.

- **Product breadcrumbs** — regularly mention the product, details of its creation, uniqueness, content, and effectiveness in your stories.

- **Cases** — share and show stories of people with different starting points who have already used the product or method, so your followers can see themselves in them and believe in their own success.

- **Sell the price** — create an expectation in the audience of a much higher price than it will actually be by showing how much it would cost the customer to achieve these results elsewhere.

- **Open cart** — a short period of time during which the warmed up audience receives the offer and the opportunity to purchase the product.

## The overarching power of storytelling

Users' attention spans have drastically shortened with the dawn of the digital age, leading to a preference for bite-sized content over lengthy texts or extended webinars. Recognizing this, internet marketers are moving away from traditional long-form sales pitches. Instead, we now deploy brief, engaging posts and stories across various days, incorporating sales messages subtly into everyday content narratives. This strategy mirrors a broader cultural shift towards short-form media, similar to how serialized TV shows captivate viewers with episodes released over months.

Drawing inspiration from this format, I've pinpointed four key instruments to capture and maintain audience interest in our digital landscape:

Storytelling — a tool that any story on social networks should be based on. Paul Zak, a specialist in neuroeconomics, conducted a study during which he proved that when we hear dry facts, our brain only engages the left hemisphere. Stories engage the right hemisphere, which generates images and emotions. This is a chemical reaction during which oxytocin, the hormone of trust, is produced. Also, thanks to storytelling, the reader associates the hero with themselves, forming an additional attachment.

The "open loop" concept, borrowed from Hollywood, makes us hooked on movies and TV shows. Our brains treat unresolved stories or cliffhangers in shows similarly to real-life unfinished situations, creating a sense of urgency and curiosity to find out what happens next. This psychological trick can be effectively used in content creation to keep the audience engaged. In order to avoid frustration, however, strategically plan climaxes like those in TV series episodes, where they naturally persuade viewers to come back for more.

**News hook:** People are often drawn to events that stand out from the ordinary—big purchases, weddings, or trips—mirroring what we frequently see in news headlines and tabloids. This raises the question: must our lives become exceptionally dramatic to garner audience interest? Not necessarily. The secret lies in the presentation.

Take baking a cake, for instance. Simply posting a photo might not spark much interest. However, turn it into a narrative—perhaps it's your first attempt at baking, inspired by your grandmother's recipe. Start by asking your audience for advice, share your emotional connection to the recipe, and take your followers along on your ingredient shopping trip, making them part of the story. The cooking process, with its challenges and suspense about the outcome, keeps them engaged. This build-up creates a perfect opportunity to introduce a product or service relevant to the story, such as fitness training programs that allow you to enjoy culinary treats without the guilt.

**Interactivity:** In the previous point, sharing an example of how to make an ordinary cake a news hook, I gave a scheme of stories, which includes a lot of requests for audience feedback.

Nobody wants to be a passive listener. We all would like to be involved, to be part of the whole, to be noticed. It's important for us to be important, a person gets particular satisfaction from feeling their own relevance. And if your warm-up makes your audience feel important and included, they will follow your blog more closely. It will give them a sense of ownership, which will greatly increase their loyalty.

To this end, I suggest you get into the habit of being interested in your audience's perspective — after all, you are running the blog for them and creating the product for them. Ask them for their opinion, to choose names and designs together. Run polls, collect advice in a window, publish screenshots of their messages, so they write even more, knowing that they are being acknowledged.

If you get it right, your warm-up will go as smoothly as a chat about life you're your best friends. As a result, your sales could triple or even tenfold thanks to the queue of eager customers coming in from social networks.

Unfortunately, one chapter is not enough to give you all the techniques with examples, but I have prepared a separate document for you in which I have collected extended lists with examples, full scenarios for warm-ups on Instagram, which you can take for yourself for free via solodar. com/instsecrets. I am confident that by following my advice, you will soon discover a new blue ocean of potential customers and be able to easily outperform your competitors.

The secret system of expert content on Instagram that brought me eight-figure sums.

# Michael Fomkin

Michael Fomkin is a distinguished Tony Award-winning Broadway investor and producer, celebrated with over 38 awards, including 6 Tonys and a Lifetime Achievement Award. He co-founded Vision Craft Course, teaching the art of video storytelling to enhance client trust and engagement. Additionally, he co-created VIP Ignite, transforming networking in the entertainment industry. Michael's entrepreneurial spirit extends to founding Truth Mgmt, a firm that elevates artists in TV, film, and fashion. His pioneering work in marketing spans over a decade, and he's committed to social causes, notably collaborating with Operation Underground Railroad to combat child trafficking. His Amazon bestseller, 'Finding Fame', showcases his expertise in blending business, entertainment, marketing, and philanthropy. Michael's career is marked by creativity, innovation, and a profound impact on individuals across diverse industries, demonstrating his unique ability to connect and empower through his ventures.

SCAN ME

# Chapter 6

# THE POWER OF STORYTELLING IN BUSINESS

**Michael Fomkin**

## *"Only those who dare to fail greatly can ever achieve greatly."*

Robert Kennedy

Hi. My name is Michael Fomkin, and I would like to share a story with you, one that I could not have imagined telling a short few years ago. It's a story filled with excitement, loss, and triumph. Now before I begin, though, let me set the tone for what I am about to share with you in this chapter.

I remember the first time I was on a main stage. It was a business conference in Las Vegas for entrepreneurs, and the host of the event called me the night before and asked if I could give a 20-minute talk on networking and following up. See, he knew my first company, VIP IGNITE, was a powerhouse in that department.

As I arrived that morning, the room was bustling with a thousand attendees, and the air was thick with excitement and hope. I was speaking in between Les Brown and Mark Victor Hanson. It felt like a gathering of kindred spirits, united by a shared anticipation that was almost cult-like in its intensity.

As I looked around, I wondered if they all felt the same electrifying excitement I did. This was the moment that would reveal to me the true power of storytelling, overshadowing even the product itself. My stomach was filled with butterflies. I remembered what Les Brown had told me earlier in the day: You will always have butterflies. You just need to learn how to have them fly in formation.

Now what happens next, that will shock you. I will save that part for later.

See, I've learned that storytelling is vital in business during my two decades working in Hollywood. Telling a story allows anyone to connect with their audience and transform their brand into more than a product or a service. Through storytelling, a business can share its values. They can also create memorable experiences that build trust and foster long-term loyalty.

"Since the dawn of humanity, we've been storytellers. From the primitive grunts of our ancestors around ancient fires, to the intricate narratives shared across the vast, interconnected web of modern technology, storytelling remains the thread that weaves through the tapestry of human existence, connecting us all on a profound level." Ancient Wisdom

How does this apply to your business, you might be thinking right now. Well, if you want to create a true brand that can stand the test of time, allow me to share this with you!

In the dynamic world of business, the art of storytelling is a cornerstone. It is central to how companies connect with their audiences. When I first came up with the concept for Vision Craft, my latest and most exciting venture, I had already recognized the transformative power of storytelling for entrepreneurs, coaches and business owners.

So, let's now begin my journey; it started with a hook— well, actually the right hook.

Hook, Story, Offer! You may have already heard the term— it's a simple framework online marketers use to gain attention online. Being a part of Russell Brunson's Inner Circle is when I first learned this concept.

Here is a definition in case you are not familiar with it.

The creators designed the "Hook, Story, offer" framework to enhance sales and marketing strategies. It was first introduced and popularized by Russell Brunson, co-founder of ClickFunnels. The framework involves capturing attention with a compelling 'Hook'. Next, engage the audience with an interesting 'Story'. Finally, present an irresistible 'Offer' to drive conversions.

That is a great framework that I use daily for my business … but if you want to not only convert but create a tribe of raving fans—aka long-term clients—you have to become a master of storytelling.

Storytelling in business is about more than selling a product/service; the goal is to create an experience that engages the audience. The experience should resonate with the values and aspirations of the audience. It's a strategic approach that humanises brands.

It turns customers into loyal advocates and shapes a company's identity in the competitive marketplace. At Vision Craft, we believe in leveraging this power. It drives engagement and growth, and creates a legacy that lingers in the hearts and minds of audiences long after the story has been told.

Working in Hollywood for almost two decades, I discovered that all great films and TV shows follow a framework called the Hero's Journey. The Hero's Journey is a narrative framework that describes the typical adventure of a hero. The hero goes beyond their ordinary world, they face challenges and finally emerge transformed. This archetypal pattern involves stages like the call to adventure, a road of trials, achieving a victory or boon, and a return home with newfound wisdom or capabilities.

As a business owner, I've discovered the transformative power of incorporating the hero's journey into my social media video content. This timeless storytelling structure helps create more than just epic tales. It's a framework that deeply resonates with my audience. I present my brand as the mentor on this journey. I guide my customers—the heroes—through their challenges, offering solutions and insights.

Each video is a chapter. In it, I address their fears; in it, I celebrate their triumphs; in it, I foster a connection that goes beyond mere transactions. I want to create stories that showcase my products or services, but I also want my stories to reflect the journey of my customers. This way, each video will be relatable and engaging. It will naturally attract leads and build lasting relationships.

As I explore the Hero's Journey, I understand its powerful impact on storytelling and personal growth. The seven key elements start with the Protagonist, that's me on my journey, facing a change in my familiar world. This leads to a Quest, a purpose or goal that drives me forward. Along the way, I find Allies, those who support and guide me. Inevitably, I encounter Challenges, obstacles that test my resolve and abilities.

These experiences lead to a Transformation, a personal change that marks my growth. Finally, there's the Legacy I leave, the impact of my journey on myself and others. Each step is integral, shaping not just a narrative.

It shapes the very essence of my personal and professional evolution.

Storytelling in business goes beyond mere communication. It serves as a vital tool to connect with audiences on a deeper level. Through the art of storytelling, companies can build trust and rapport, make their brand more approachable, and make their messages more memorable. It's about creating a connection that touches people's emotions and values, not just sharing facts and figures.

As a business owner, I've realized that a powerful story can truly engage an audience. It makes complex concepts more understandable and persuasive. It helps differentiate my brand in a crowded marketplace. It creates a unique identity that customers can relate to. I can communicate my company's purpose and vision by harnessing the power of storytelling. It engages customers in a way that factual presentations simply cannot.

This approach aids in marketing and brand building. It also aids in internal communication, fostering a strong company culture and shared values among team members. The psychology of storytelling in marketing taps into the human brain's natural inclination for narratives.

It offers a profound way to connect with consumers on a deeper, more emotional level.

This approach to marketing goes beyond product promotion. It creates stories that resonate with audiences and evoke emotional responses. It promotes a personal connection with the brand. The strategic integration of storytelling into marketing engages our emotions, which in turn makes products and services more memorable and appealing.

Emotional engagement plays a key role in capturing attention, fostering loyalty, and building trust. Consumers tend to remember and connect with brands that use storytelling well, as these narratives often reflect their own experiences or aspirations. By leveraging the psychological power of storytelling, brands can forge a unique identity and stand out in a crowded marketplace. This strategic differentiation helps them cultivate lasting relationships with their audiences. The art of storytelling in marketing involves creating a persuasive brand narrative that audiences can believe in and aspire to be a part of.

Here are three examples to illustrate how you can craft your narrative effectively:

The Origin Story: This narrative focuses on the roots of your business. For instance, let's say you started a coffee shop. Your narrative might revolve around your passion for coffee, inspired by your travels to coffee farms in Colombia, where you learned about the art of coffee making. This journey led to the birth of your coffee shop, which aims to bring authentic and sustainable coffee to the community. This story emphasizes your deep connection to the product and your commitment to sustainability.

The Challenge Overcome: This narrative highlights a significant challenge your business faced and how you overcame it. For example, imagine you run a tech start-up that initially struggled with software development. Your narrative could detail the hurdles you faced, the late nights, and the breakthrough moment that led to your innovative software solution. This story showcases perseverance, innovation, and the ability to overcome obstacles.

The Customer-Centric Approach: This narrative centers on how your business has positively impacted customers. Suppose you have a fitness app. Your narrative could focus on stories of how your app has transformed the lives of individuals—from someone who regained fitness post-pregnancy to another who found a community through your app's social features. This story doesn't just sell a product; it demonstrates real-world impact and builds an emotional connection with your audience.

 In each example, the key is to connect emotionally, highlight authentic experiences and showcase the values and mission that drive your business. This approach to storytelling helps build a more relatable and memorable brand identity.

 Now underneath these stories are 13 other stories that, when told in sequence, will get your ideal customer to know, like, trust and buy from you. Not just buy, but become raving fans of your products and services. This will always lead to a windfall of profits and cash flow for anyone who follows this formula.

 That is why I created Vision Craft—to help entrepreneurs create their ideal client indoctrination sequence from storyboards to actually filming on a multi-million dollar sound stage.

One other tip I give entrepreneurs is to always have the right photos done. We call our shoots the Heroic Visionary Package. We will shoot over 500 photos to establish the person as a thought leader. Everything from styling to wardrobe is handled by the former art director of Vogue Magazine.

When preparing for a photoshoot like the "Heroic Visionary Package," here are some tips I always start out with.

Define Your Brand's Image: Understand the message you want to convey through the photos. This should align with your brand's ethos and the perception you would like to create among your audience.

Choose Appropriate Attire: We work with professional stylists, like those from Vogue, to select outfits that reflect your brand colors and personality. Your attire should be consistent with how you would present yourself to your ideal clients.

Plan the Shoot Details: Decide on locations, poses, and themes that best represent your brand. This could include a mix of formal, casual, and action shots to provide a well-rounded portrayal of your personal and professional persona.

Communicate with Your Photographer: Ensure your photographer understands your brand and the style of photos you need. Clear communication will help in achieving the desired outcome. This is something we go over in our course before the shoot.

Relax and Be Authentic: During the shoot, try to be natural and authentic. Authenticity resonates well on social media and helps in forming a genuine connection with your audience. We actually have an Emmy award-winning actor train our clients on stage presence and bring in published models to work on posing in front of the camera.

Remember, these photos are a long-term investment in your brand's image, so taking the time to prepare and execute them well is essential. These images become a brand representation of the person they are destined to be.

Entrepreneurs require an unfair advantage when it comes to understanding how to turn casual browsers into paying customers in today's social media world. Obviously, storytelling and brand imagery are the first steps. Here are some other methods I've used.

Narrow your niche and create content that resonates deeply with your audience, building trust and relevance. Offer value upfront through free resources or insights. This is a powerful way to attract attention and start nurturing potential leads. Consistently engaging with your audience through interactive and tailored content turns passive viewers into active participants, fostering a sense of community and loyalty.

Focusing on excellent customer service on social media platforms will not only set you apart from your competition, but also help establish credibility, grow your following, and build a strong brand reputation.

Remember, a well-crafted social media marketing strategy should aim to not only capture attention but also to maintain it, turning followers into brand advocates and, ultimately, into paying clients.

 To conclude, the journey of storytelling in business that I have experienced and shared with you is testimony to the profound power and impact it holds. From the bright lights of a Las Vegas stage to the nuanced strategies of online marketing, storytelling is proving to be the ultimate tool for connecting, persuading and transforming. As we continue to pursue our entrepreneurial ambitions, it is important to remember that our stories are not just narratives. They are the very core of our brands and our personal journeys.

The art of storytelling, whether through the Hook, Story, Offer framework, the timeless Hero's Journey or the authentic narratives we incorporate into our marketing campaigns, is the heartbeat of effective business communication. It allows us to reach our audiences on a deeper, more emotional level, creating lasting bonds and turning casual scrollers into loyal customers and advocates.

As we come to the end of this chapter, let's fully embrace the impact of storytelling, not only as a business tactic but as a fundamental aspect of our lives. Creating stories that deeply connect and motivate can result in personal and professional advancement. Storytelling is more than just a skill; it's an art form that, when perfected, has the power to take your business to greater heights and create a lasting legacy.

Remember, in the world of business, your story is your strength. It's what sets you apart from the competition, what connects you to your audience, and what propels you forward. Embrace your narrative, share it with the world, and watch as it transforms your business and those it touches.

To learn more about us and how we can help you 10x your leads through video storytelling, please visit http://www.visioncraftcourse.com

# Ryan Thompson

Ryan Thompson has achieved remarkable success in sales and marketing, climbing the ranks from a rookie to a champion and eventually becoming a multi-business owner. With an illustrious career spanning three different industries over 30 years, Ryan's expertise is unparalleled. Connect with him at realestatebrilliance.com.au

A decade ago, he established Real Estate Brilliance, a training and coaching company aimed at assisting agents and offices to achieve similar success as to what he achieved, just much quicker. Ryan created The Agent Success System, a step by step, rubber to road program empowering agents and agencies to fast track their success in the real estate industry. Through these initiatives, Ryan has impacted the lives of countless agents, introducing two additional programs: Team You Incorporated, for those seeking team growth and scalability, and Leadership and Business Management for Real Estate, a comprehensive guide to running a thriving real estate agency.

Ryan's true passion lies in helping agents and agencies unlock their full potential, enabling them to lead extraordinary lives. Connect with him at realestatebrilliance.com.au

SCAN ME

# Chapter 7

# WHO WANTS TO BE A SALES CHAMPION?

**Ryan Thompson**

## *"If it's to be, it is up to me"*
William Johnsen

So, you've decided to dive into the world of sales, thinking it's a sure-fire way to achieve everlasting success and piles of cash. I mean, how hard could it be, right? With my smooth-talking skills and a sprinkle of charm, I thought I had it all figured out. Boy, was I wrong. Turns out, there are two types of sales paths, and I started with the easy one, thinking that's all there was.

Internal sales, where people stroll into a store looking for a fridge, and the salesperson just has to point out the price differences and convince them they can't live without the fanciest model. If you're a lousy salesperson, you just let them figure it out themselves, but they still end up leaving with a new fridge. Piece of cake, right? Well, that's where I started, and I thought I was the best damn salesperson out there. I made sure everyone knew it too. I was unstoppable. So, naturally, I decided to venture into the world of commission-only sales because that's where the real money was. And boy, was I awesome...

Now, external sales, the kind where there are no limits to what you can achieve. They say you can "write your own check" at the end of each month. Take real estate sales, for example. You have to go out there and find houses to sell. First, you have to find someone who actually wants to sell their house. Then, you have to convince them that you're better than all the other agents in a 20 km radius. And trust me, there are plenty of agents to compete with, including the one who sold them the damn house in the first place, plus their three real estate agent friends. This is a whole different ball game, trust me, and it's not as easy as it sounds. This is the path I chose, and let me tell you, it was tough. A real wake-up call.

I was given a desk and a phone, and told to make it happen. No income for the first six months, and my bank account was running dry. I was struggling, and there seemed to be no easy fix. I asked around the office, and everyone had their own methods of generating leads, but none of them seemed to be working. Cold calling, email, direct mail – none of it was bringing in significant success. I was baffled. That's when I made a vow to myself – I would make it in this business or die trying.

They say, "When you go looking, they will come knocking." Once I made the decision to expand my knowledge and skills, I started attracting like-minded individuals who were also on a quest for success. They introduced me to self-help sales and marketing books, authors, and life-changing training courses that completely transformed my mindset. As I implemented the strategies I learned, I saw rapid progress in my career, finances, relationships – my entire life. I had stumbled upon something that not only helped me but also ignited a fire within me. Something just clicked. I discovered the unbelievable power of the mind and how it can shape your life when you choose to think positively and make a change. This curiosity and dedication to my craft propelled me to achieve greatness in my sales career. I became a sales champion, a sales and marketing director for multiple businesses, and a performance coach and trainer. I even wrote three training programs and created countless practical systems that have helped thousands of agents reach their full potential and live extraordinary lives. And most importantly, I found true happiness and fulfillment in my own life.

So, I've been asked to share a topic with you, and I've chosen the one that set me on this incredible journey – demystifying the marketing matrix. Let's talk about all those prospecting and marketing tasks and activities. Which ones actually work? Which ones give you a quick return on investment? And which ones can you just leave for later? We'll dive into the ones that cost money and the ones that are more about return on effort and energy – meaning they're practically free. I'll reveal the strategies you absolutely can't afford to skip and the ones you can toss out the window.

Get ready because I'm about to spill the beans….. Welcome to THE PROSPECTING AND MARKETING SPEEDOMETER.

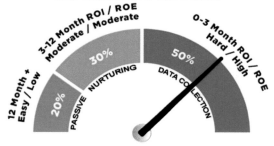

The prospecting and marketing speedometer is an analogy that everyone can relate to — the speedometer and performance of their cars. Just like stepping on the accelerator increases the car's performance, stepping up your prospecting and marketing activities improves your business. On the other hand, if you press down lightly onto the accelerator, the car's performance is moderate. And if you take your foot off the accelerator completely, the car stands still. This analogy applies to your business as well. Your business is the car, the acceleration represents your prospecting and marketing activities, and the engine's performance is your return on investment or return on effort (ROI or ROE)

Now that we have a tool to measure the effectiveness of our prospecting and marketing activities, let's examine the diagram and break down the three sections in detail. On the far right, we have the RED section, which signifies high revs and optimal performance. So, what does this mean for our business?

## PART 2: THE RED SECTION

In the realm of prospecting and marketing, the RED SECTION is where things start to happen quickly. These activities, when executed meticulously and consistently, offer rapid returns within a three-month period. However, they come with their fair share of challenges and intimidation, often pushing individuals out of their comfort zones or requiring significant financial investment. Not everyone is equipped to handle these tasks, which is why they are not widely pursued. After all, if it were easy, everyone would be doing it, right?

## THE COMMUNITY BUILDING PHASE

The RED SECTION also represents the phase of community building. Personally, I find the term "Database" to be impersonal. Instead, I prefer to refer to it as a "Community" since it evokes a sense of belonging and togetherness. The first step in any business venture is to establish a strong community. This is especially crucial for newcomers, as it lays the foundation for ongoing business opportunities. It is essential to put in the hard work and focus on building a community to extract business from into the future.

Unfortunately, it is not the norm for individuals and businesses to spend most of their time and resources in THE RED SECTION, outperforming their competition. Instead, many businesses operate reactively, without a solid plan in place. They only dip into this zone sporadically, struggling to stay afloat rather than building a strong community and fostering enduring relationships.

## SOME EXAMPLES OF RED ACTIVITIES

**1. Face-to-Face, Door-to-Door, or Business-to-Business:** albeit it may seem old-fashioned, there is still to this day no better way to get sales now or create contacts for future sales. It is crucial to approach the initial meeting as an opportunity to establish a connection and ignite the relationship process, rather than an opportunity to sell your product or service. If on the off chance your timing is perfect, and your prospect is, in fact, ready to buy your product or service there and then, this is just a bonus. Building rapport and gaining favor with potential clients is the primary goal. While this approach may seem intimidating, it is an excellent way to build a community, and the best part is, it's free! All it requires is your time and a friendly demeanor. Consider bringing a small gift, like a Kit-Kat, to break the ice. Surprisingly, most people are polite and willing to listen to your pitch, allowing you to stay in touch with them. They understand the challenges of this method and appreciate your efforts. (100% cut through or leave a card/voucher).

**2. Social Media Paid Ads:** A more modern approach to building your community, or for those products or services that allow you to reach far and wide. Paid advertising, especially on social media platforms, can be highly effective and has no boundaries, only limited to your budget and resources. The advantage of social media ads is that you can track the analytics of every ad and measure the return on investment (ROI). It is important to note that social media marketing is not a quick fix. It requires expertise or the assistance of someone who knows the ins and outs of this strategy. You can compare it to a fishing trawler, dragging its net on the ocean floor and picking up not just fish but also debris. While there may be some qualified leads, most of it is unqualified. Therefore, you must sift through the debris to find the fish, which can be hard work resembling cold calling. Building a healthy community takes time and effort.

**3. Lead Magnets with Opt-Ins:** Utilizing the law of reciprocity, offering something of value for free, such as a book, e-book, webinar, or coaching session, can encourage prospects to opt-in. This gives you the opportunity to win their business in the short term or nurture them to serve their needs in the future.

**4. SEO:** Depending on the competitiveness of your industry and your budget, investing in search engine optimization (SEO) can be a fantastic way to generate inquiries and build your community. However, it can be costly, and success requires expertise and well-defined search criteria.

In conclusion, THE RED SECTION is where the real action happens. It requires dedication, strategic planning, and a willingness to step out of your comfort zone. By focusing on community building and implementing effective marketing activities, you can outperform your competition and lay the foundation for long-term success. Regardless of which method or combination you choose, never forget the red section is for making the CONNECTION, then building the relationship accordingly.

### THE ORANGE SECTION (nurturing phase)

Imagine your business is now like a smooth-running engine, cruising along at a moderate pace. You're no longer pushing the pedal to the floor, but instead, you're maintaining a steady speed. In this phase, it's crucial to stay in touch with your potential clients and nurture the community you've built. By keeping them informed and engaged, you can increase brand awareness and become the first choice when they need a product or service like yours. The activities in this phase may seem more manageable and administrative, but they require skill, dedication, and consistency to yield results. While the return on investment may take 3–12 months, the great thing about these activities is that they can be automated and measured with the right systems in place.

## Some Examples of activities in the orange phase:

**1. Email Marketing:** Utilize electronic direct mail, such as newsletters, to provide value-added information, product updates, or giveaways. While email open rates may be low, loyal email users who find your content engaging will support your business and even refer you to others. The key is to focus on quality content rather than frequency, making emails personal and authentic. (18-25% open rate/cut through)

**2. Direct Mail:** Similar to email marketing, direct mail can be used to share valuable content. However, it can be costly and requires obtaining the recipient's address, which could be difficult to obtain. However, if you are able to and you have the budget for, it does get lots of eyes on your messaging, building great connection. (80% open rate/cut through)

2.1. Chunk Mail — Consider sending chunky mail, such as packages or envelopes with unique items like key rings or magnets, to increase open rates. Albeit quite costly, if you nail the item and it is useful, it could remain in eye shot, or, as they say, have shelf life for a long time to come. (95% open rate/cut through)

**3. Letterbox Dropping:** Flyers or pamphlets can catch your target audience's attention and create a brief moment of engagement. By providing valuable information or exclusive offers or even gift vouchers, you can increase the chances of them paying attention and keeping your materials for future reference. Consistency is key in this method, as it takes time to establish recognition and trust. (50% potential for air time/cut through)

**4. Sponsorship/Networking:** While this activity involves face-to-face interaction, it falls under the orange phase due to its slow-burn nature. Building relationships and becoming the preferred supplier for clubs, teams, or networking groups requires ongoing participation and personal involvement. It's not just about placing logos or making tax write-offs; it's about genuinely engaging with the community. This is where we show them, we're human and care.

**5. Community Seasonal Campaigns:** Interacting with the wider community and your own self-built Community, through events or competitions, can strengthen your brand and foster a sense of belonging. Involving children in activities like treasure hunts or coloring competitions can capture attention and create a positive association with your brand. Not to mention a terrific give to get investment.

**6. Voice to Voice Nurture Calls:** While calling someone may seem daunting, it provides an opportunity to have a personal conversation and offer valuable information or deals. Even if they don't answer, leaving a personal message with some useful information warms the relationship for future encounters. In my opinion, a call every 6 months is mandatory if you truly want to build relationships.

**7. Text Messaging:** Text messages can be an effective way to communicate with your audience, as they can respond at their convenience. However, it's crucial to provide valuable information or incentives to maintain their interest. If your target audience has been well communicated with and is familiar with you, texting could be a great way to get them to opt in for a red-hot deal or seasonal promotion. If they are not warm, they may unsubscribe, and you have lost them on text forever.

**8. Thank You Cards, anniversary cards or birthday cards:** Building rapport and winning favor can still be achieved through old-fashioned strategies like sending cards. The power of a simple card should not be underestimated. Sending physical cards through snail mail adds an emotional connection and shows your commitment to building relationships. The key to this or any stretch is when you start you never stop as it has a compounding event and continues to grow in interest and dividends.

## GREEN PHASE (passive marketing phase)

In the green phase, your business is idling along, neither revving high nor cruising. It serves as a reminder and reinforcement of your brand, positioning, and market dominance. However, the prospecting and marketing activities in this phase have an extended return on investment (12 months plus if ever) and are difficult to measure. While these activities may not involve much effort on your behalf or are within your comfort zone, they should not be the primary focus of your marketing plan or consume most of your precious resources.

**Some examples of activities in the green phase:**

**1. Visual Signage:** Traditional signboards, billboards, and ads on buses or bus stops can be hard to ignore. They serve as a visual reminder of your brand and can trigger needs and wants through subliminal messaging. However, this space is expensive and challenging to calculate ROI, making it more suitable for companies with large marketing budgets.

**2. Content Creation:** Creating blogs, editorials, advertorials, and free social media posts is essential in today's fast-paced marketing world. Regularly generating fresh and engaging content across multiple channels is crucial for getting noticed and recognized. While it's important to care about the content you create, don't overthink it. Share what catches your interest, and if it resonates with your audience, amplify it further. Although this is an essential task and has no direct ROI, it does form part of the overall marketing machine as it feeds most activities.

Creating Your Very Own Multi Layered Prospecting system (MLPS)

Now that you understand the different phases and activities, it's time to create the MLPS that suits your business, goals, ambitions, and resources. Consider incorporating a mix of activities from each phase. If your business is new or lacks a community, focus on more red activities. If you already have a healthy community, prioritize nurturing activities. If you're well-known and have a strong following, green activities can reinforce your brand. Remember, your system is dynamic and can change based on your success. There are no rules or limits to how much ground you cover or how much you invest; the only limits are the ones you place on yourself. Stay consistent and never stop striving for success.

# Multi Layered Prospecting System

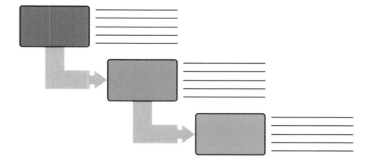

# Kew Jaliens

Kew Jaliens is a former professional footballer and mindset coach from the Netherlands. He had a successful career as a central defender, playing for renowned clubs such as Sparta Rotterdam, Willem II, and AZ Alkmaar. Jaliens also had international experience, representing the Netherlands at the 2006 FIFA World Cup and the 2008 Beijing Olympics. After retiring from professional football, he transitioned into mindset coaching, utilizing his knowledge and experience to help athletes and entrepreneurs unlock their full potential. Jaliens is passionate about mental strength and believes that a strong mindset is crucial for success in sports and life. Through his coaching, he aims to empower individuals to overcome challenges, build resilience, and achieve their goals. Jaliens' unique combination of football expertise and mindset coaching makes him a valuable resource for athletes and entrepreneurs seeking to enhance their performance.

SCAN ME

# Chapter 8

# THE EIGHT PILLARS OF MINDSET

**Kew Jaliens**

> *"Mindset change is not about picking up a few pointers here and there. It's about seeing things in a new way. When people...change to a growth mindset, they change from a judge-and-be-judged framework to a learn-and-help-learn framework. Their commitment is to growth, and growth takes plenty of time, effort, and mutual support."*
>
> Carol Dweck

With a career that stretched across two decades, I, have truly lived the dream of professional football. As a player of Surinamese and African descent born in Rotterdam, Netherlands, I journeyed across various clubs in my native country and abroad. Playing predominantly as a central defender, I spent over a decade dedicating my craft to AZ Alkmaar, making over 250 appearances and winning the Dutch Cup in 2013.

My playing career also included stints with other prominent clubs like Willem II, Wisła Kraków, and Newcastle Jets. One of my proudest honors was representing the Netherlands at the international level. I earned 10 caps playing for my country, including competing at the 2006 FIFA World Cup and 2008 Beijing Olympics.

After retiring from professional football in 2016, I transitioned into off-field roles like serving as Academy Director at Newcastle Jets and Technical Director for NNSW Football. Presently, I work as a Mindset Coach, drawing from my breadth of experiences to help individuals unlock their potential.

The journey towards success is shaped by various factors, but none is as pivotal as an individual's mindset. The beliefs, attitudes, and thoughts that make up one's mindset determine how they approach challenges, seize opportunities, and navigate their path. As a former professional football player and current mindset coach, I have created a comprehensive framework of eight pillars that influence and shape a person's mindset. These pillars—which include discipline, health, spirituality, relationships, obligation and charity, fear and risk, goals, and money—provide a profound blueprint for personal growth and achievement.

The impact of mindset on one's success and achievements are profound. As I've experienced firsthand, individuals who nurture a growth mindset tend to achieve more. This is due to their heightened resilience, motivation, and willingness to dedicate the necessary effort to surmount obstacles and attain goals. Conversely, a fixed mindset can restrict potential and impede personal and professional growth by fostering avoidance of challenges and fear of failure. My coaching aims to help people unlock their potential by cultivating empowering mindsets oriented towards growth.

Psychologist Carol Dweck's ground-breaking work defines two main types of mindsets: growth and fixed. A fixed mindset assumes that talents and abilities are inherent and unalterable, leading to avoidance of challenges and a fear of failure. On the other hand, a growth mindset embraces the idea that effort, learning, and perseverance can lead to the development of skills and talents. This distinction forms the foundation for how individuals approach their aspirations and challenges.

Mindset encompasses an individual's beliefs, attitudes, and thoughts that shape their behaviors and perceptions of the world. It acts as the lens through which people interpret and respond to various life situations and challenges. Two prominent mindsets shape our approach to life: the fixed mindset and the growth mindset:

**1. Fixed Mindset:** This kind of mindset affirms that abilities, intelligence, and talents are inherent traits that cannot be altered. Individuals with a fixed mindset tend to evade challenges, abandon efforts easily, and consider failures as reflections of their inadequacies. They seek validation and shy away from taking risks.

**2. Growth Mindset:** In contrast, the growth mindset asserts that abilities can be cultivated through effort, practice, and learning. People with this mindset embrace challenges, persevere in the face of setbacks, and view failures as stepping stones toward personal development. They are more inclined to take risks and exhibit a positive attitude toward learning and self-improvement.

## Mindset and Success Correlation

The impact of mindset on one's success and achievements are profound. Individuals who nurture a growth mindset tend to achieve more. This is as a result of their heightened resilience, motivation, and willingness to dedicate the necessary effort to surmount obstacles and attain goals. On the contrary, a fixed mindset can restrict potential and impede personal and professional growth.

## The Journey of Discovery

For much of my football career, I was oblivious of the concept of mindset, let alone the distinctions between growth and fixed mindsets. It was only a few years back during a conversation with a 'top athlete supervisor' at my former club, AZ Alkmaar, that I first encountered the idea of mindset. At the time, we were discussing a young player grappling with the aftermath of on-field mistakes. This conversation marked the beginning of my fascination with mindset dynamics. It instigated me to research further, ultimately inspiring my transition into coaching focused specifically on cultivating empowering mindsets.

## Beyond the Growth Mindset

The pivotal question that took root in my mind was whether a growth mindset alone determined my successful football career, or whether other factors played a role.

This drove my more in-depth research into the pillars that shape achievement.

**The Eight Pillars of Influences on Mindset:** Through my experience and learnings, I have distilled my insights into eight pillars that collectively shape an individual's mindset. These pillars foster the conditions for multidimensional success across various areas of life.

**1. Discipline — The Foundation of Determination and Accountability:** Discipline lays the foundation for personal growth and success. One of my formative experiences with discipline came from my father at the age of 15. I had an early morning training session after a late-night family party. I'd planned on sleeping in and skipping training, but my father, however, had other plans for me. He woke me up with a splash of water and said, "If you want to be a man at night, be a man in the morning." This principle has guided me ever since, especially as it emphasizes on the critical elements that nurture discipline—determination and accountability.

**2. Health — Nurturing Physical and Mental Well-being:** Optimal health, encompassing physical fitness, nutrition, and overall well-being, is vital for consistent high performance. My professional sports background vividly illustrates the importance of maintaining physical health to achieve peak performance during critical moments. The discipline required to fuel and train my body properly allowed me to maximize my potential when it mattered most on the pitch. The lessons apply broadly — our minds can only thrive to the extent our bodies and health support them.

**3. Spirituality — Cultivating Love, Honesty, and Gratitude:** Spirituality centers on fostering a positive mindset through qualities like love, honesty, and gratitude. My personal journey underscores the transformative power of gratitude in shaping one's overall mindset and perspective.

After losing a close family elder when I was 18, seeing the struggles of illness opened my eyes. I realized how lucky I was to play football and to simply be alive. From then on, I started each day by being grateful—for life, health, and the opportunity to do what I love. This changed how I faced everything that came after.

**4. Relationships — The Power of Meaningful Connections:** I highlight the great significance of nurturing relationships with family, friends, and partners. These connections provide both emotional support and contribute profoundly to personal growth and success. My insights reflect the idea that accomplishments are often the collective result of the family, teammates, coaches, and communities that surround us—rather than purely individual efforts alone. My achievements would not have been possible without meaningful relationships lifting me up along the way.

**5. Obligation and Charity — Giving Back and Finding Purpose:** Imagine your gift or talent as a seed that you've nurtured into a strong, fruitful tree. You could pluck all the fruits for yourself and your family, enjoying the bounty until the tree eventually stops bearing fruit. But consider a different approach, one rooted in obligation and charity: you share the seeds.

### The Gift of Giving Back

Once you've reaped the fruits of your labor, take some of the seeds and share them with others. Assist them in nurturing and cultivating their own seeds until they grow into bountiful trees. By doing so, you're enriching your life and contributing to the well-being and success of others.

### The Pillar of Obligation and Charity

This principle emphasizes the profound impact of community contribution and altruistic behavior. It's not merely about the act of giving, but about fostering an ecosystem of growth, compassion, and collective well-being.

I strongly advocate for this notion of giving back, underlining its transformative power. Rather than hoarding your success, you have the chance to enable the success of others. By investing in the community, you're not just fulfilling an obligation but adding layers of purpose and meaning to your own life and those around you.

In summary, the act of giving back enhances your personal growth journey as well as amplifies the growth potential of everyone around you. It turns the spotlight from 'me' to 'we,' creating a ripple effect of positive impact that far exceeds the boundaries of individual accomplishment. By embracing obligation and charity as integral components of personal growth, we can collectively create a richer, more harmonious world for all to thrive in. My dream is to empower others by sharing the lessons that propelled my own success and fulfillment.

### 6. Fear and Risk — Embracing Challenges for Growth:

First and foremost, allow me to clarify something: fear and risk are not your enemies. Rather, they are crucial indicators, signposts on the road to personal development. They aren't there to complicate your journey; they are there to show you where you need to go to grow.

### How to navigate fear?

Fear often creeps in when you're about to do something significant—especially when you're on the biggest stages. As a former professional football player, I can tell you that thoughts like "What if we lose?" or "What if I make a mistake?" are completely natural. But here's how I used to handle them:

I'd return to square one and count my blessings. Realizing the unique position I was in—to be able to play at that level—filled me with gratitude. Instead of succumbing to fear,

I'd ask myself, "What if we win? What if I play an amazing game?" This shift in perspective frequently transformed my fear into positive energy and drive, propelling me to give my best.

## Calculated risks — Steppingstones to success

Now let's talk about risks. Risks are like toll booths on your highway to success. You can't get to where you're going without passing through them. Truth is, taking calculated risks is not an option; it's a requirement. By doing so, you liberate yourself from the stagnation that comfort zones offer and open doors to significant growth opportunities.

## The importance of Resilience

One of the most valuable outcomes of confronting your fears and taking risks is the resilience you build along the way. I often refer to this process as 'life's training ground.' It's where you learn that setbacks, failures, and challenges aren't the end of the world; they are valuable lessons. And lessons, if learned well, make you stronger, wiser, and more equipped to deal with whatever comes next. So, embracing fear and taking calculated risks within the framework of a growth mindset are more than self-help buzzwords; they are actionable principles that can help you lead a fulfilling life. By making these practices an integral part of your personal development journey, you'll find that the challenges you face become opportunities for growth, propelling you closer to your goals.

By understanding and applying these insights, you are not just surviving; you're thriving. And isn't that what we're all aiming for?

**7. Goals — A Framework for Clear Objectives:** When I was 20 years old, I'd just secured a significant transfer and found myself sitting across from my new coach. He asked me, "What are your goals and aspirations? Where do you see yourself in a couple of years?" I responded without hesitation: "I see myself in the Dutch national team." It may have seemed audacious at the time—there was no concrete evidence to suggest I would reach that level. Yet, that was the vision I had for myself, and the goal I set. The lesson here is that if the destiny is in place, the route doesn't matter.

## The Roadmap to Success

Setting goals is like having a GPS for your life's journey. They help you navigate decisions that align with your objectives, ensuring you don't drift aimlessly and miss opportunities for growth and improvement.

## The Power of Focus

Goals help to channel your time and resources effectively. They direct your efforts, helping you discard distractions that do not serve your primary objectives.

## Accountability Through Goal setting

There's something about writing down your goals and perhaps sharing them with others, which brings about a sense of accountability. This personal responsibility becomes a powerful motivator, fuelling a disciplined approach toward achieving your ambitions.

## Measurable Outcomes

The SMART (Specific, Measurable, Achievable, Relevant, and Time-bound) framework provides a structure that allows you to track your progress. It offers critical feedback for understanding what's working and what isn't, allowing you the flexibility to adjust your strategies for better outcomes.

## Resilience and Adaptability

When you are goal-oriented, you're naturally subjecting yourself to challenges, setbacks, and failures. But if you adopt a growth mindset, you see these as invaluable opportunities for learning and adaptation. The pursuit of goals acts as a resilience-training ground, teaching you to be adaptable in the face of changing circumstances.

**Boosting Self-Efficacy and Confidence**

Accomplishing smaller goals boosts your confidence and reinforces the belief that you're capable of achieving even greater things. This sense of competence feeds back positively into your growth mindset, inspiring you to take on bigger challenges.

**A Purpose-Driven Life**

Goals help to infuse your daily activities with meaning and purpose. Having a sense of purpose is vital for maintaining your motivation and enthusiasm, both of which are key elements for nurturing a growth mindset.

**Continual Learning**

Goal setting also encourages a learning orientation. Each goal achieved sets the stage for a higher, more challenging goal. This cycle fosters perpetual learning and improvement, foundational pillars of a growth mindset.

In essence, goal setting and a growth mindset are closely intertwined. Goals provide the structure, metrics, and challenges that fuel the behavior and attitudes crucial for a growth mindset, such as resilience and focus. In turn, a growth mindset can make the process of setting and achieving goals more effective and fulfilling. So remember, set your goals high—because if you can see it, you can be it!

**8. Money — Managing Resources for Holistic Success:** While financial success is a common aspiration, I emphasize that money is just one element of the success equation. Wise financial management combined with investments in personal growth, relationships, and charitable endeavors showcases the interconnectedness of these eight pillars and their collective impact. True fulfillment requires balancing all aspects of life — career, family, community, health, and spirituality.

## The Nexus of Mindset and Entrepreneurship

Entrepreneurs, often endowed with a growth mindset, exhibit a familiarity with overcoming adversity and leveraging challenges to fuel growth. However, it is essential for entrepreneurs to cultivate a mindset that matches their aspirations and ambitions, scaling their personal growth alongside their business endeavors.

## Conclusion: The Mindset Framework to Nurture Growth and Become Your Best Self

My journey from professional football into coaching underscores the transformative power of mindset in shaping achievement. By identifying the eight pillars influencing mindset, I present a comprehensive roadmap for unlocking potential. By embracing a growth mindset and cultivating these pillars, we can effectively navigate challenges, surmount setbacks, and forge paths to multidimensional success. My insights demonstrate that personal growth is a lifelong voyage guided by discipline, self-awareness, and continuous learning. The interplay of these pillars serves as a testament to the integral role of mindset in sculpting a flourishing life of meaning and purpose. My goal is to empower others to manifest their greatness.

# Hassan Varasi

Hassan Varasi, with an MBA and over a decade of experience, is a distinguished managing director known for his strategic expertise across the digital, real estate, and product development sectors, particularly within Asian markets. His leadership at Plusco Tech Asia, Plusco Realstate, and Plusco Australia has been pivotal in driving growth and facilitating significant transactions and developments. His career began with a transformative role at Cool Or Cosy, where he innovated the solar rental concept, significantly boosting the company's turnover within a year. Hassan's journey reflects a blend of innovation, strategic vision, and operational excellence, with skills in direct sales, startup leadership, and international project management. Based in Fort Lauderdale, Florida, he continues to impact the business world through his roles, where his work transcends traditional boundaries, combining market insight with a commitment to sustainability and customer satisfaction. His path from sales representative to executive positions showcases a dynamic career built on resilience, adaptability, and a forward-thinking mindset.

# Chapter 9

# STRATEGIC PRODUCT INNOVATION FOR START-UPS

**Hassan Varasi**

A decade of experience in product innovation and development in Asia has shown me that Chinese manufacturers are the most efficient, dependable, capable, and easiest to work with of any other manufacturers I've attempted to engage to build things. The new product developers required to precisely define the product needs in their market with Chinese manufacturing partners, emphasizing quality, functionality, colours, and packaging.

China produces vast quantities of items for overseas clients, and the influx of purchasers allows Chinese manufacturers to focus on mass production and bulk packaging. Chinese sophisticated economic policies, which have been implemented since the 1980s, have resulted in manufacturing endowment factors in numerous industries that no other country can match. These tremendous endowment elements have transformed China into the global hub of product sourcing.

But what has China's excellence in low-cost manufacturing got to do with a chapter on strategic product innovation, you might ask?

And the answer is: everything. If you're setting up a product development start-up, you need to think about how you're going to manufacture and distribute your products from the outset. China's manufacturing expertise plays a big part in this, as do the country's strengths in speed to market, access to a wide variety of suppliers and materials, and the scalability of your efforts when working with manufacturing partners in China. What's more, an often overlooked element is that, in addition to being the world's manufacturing powerhouse, China is rapidly becoming a thriving innovation ecosystem.

Let's start at the beginning and a short introduction into the most important elements of product development and innovation.

The terms refer to the creation and introduction of

a product or service that is new to the market or a significant improvement to an existing product. It includes improvements in components and technical specifications, as well as functional characteristics such as ease of use. Product innovation falls into three main categories, as discussed below.

## 1. New product innovation

New products are defined as either radical or disruptive because, if they achieve a successful adoption rate, they can become game changers and cause a market shift. However, radical and disruptive innovations are difficult to get right, have a lower success rate and carry more risk. The success of new products therefore requires a systematic and disciplined approach. proven strategy to transform ideas from conception to marketable products.

## 2. Incremental changes of existing products

Incremental innovation aims to improve existing products. It is the most lucrative and successful type of product innovation because it improves products that are already successful in the marketplace. It also meets the needs of consumers - for example, the innovation of the computer into smartphones, laptops, tablets and PCs.

## 3. Development of new product features

Introducing new product features is the third type of product innovation. Developers and designers create new features to improve products and increase their frequency and acceptance. The purpose is to maintain the original usability and utility of the product.

## The benefit of Product innovation

Product innovation is essential for business growth. Consumer needs and desires are evolving, and technology is improving at lightning speed. It is vital that a company continually innovates to remain relevant in the marketplace. Product and service innovation directly improves a company's quality and performance.

Innovation facilitates change and therefore increases the efficiency and effectiveness of business processes. Innovation enables companies to make more effective use of the product differentiation strategy, creating a unique offering and competitive advantage.

Strategic product innovation enables companies to generate profits. For example, companies can dominate the market by taking a holistic approach, such as developing a new product and/or incrementally improving existing products. For example, Apple dominates the global smartphone market by maintaining a competitive advantage through incremental improvements in the features and functionality of existing products.

The whole aim of product innovation is therefore, to gain a competitive advantage in the market.

**Strategic Product innovation**

Unlike the traditional product development method, which requires a team of professional product developers and marketing experts with substantial financial resources to investigate a sophisticated three-step product development process, the strategic product innovation process builds on a market-leading product that is already experiencing successful market adoption. For example, startups and new entrepreneurs may not have sufficient financial and human resources to develop a product using the traditional method and grow a business at the same time. As a result, the traditional product development process is considered unprofitable or unattainable for most people.

In the strategic process of product development, entrepreneurs need to identify a leading product that dominates the market with remarkable success. On this basis, they can then develop a product with a similar function or innovate to improve the product's performance and functionality. In both cases, the design had to follow the basic framework of the leading products. It is important that the improved version of the existing product retains most of the features of the original product to remain relevant to consumers' perceptions. However, the new products must not infringe the trademark, patent and design protection of the market-leading product.

## How to develop products with a minimum budget

Today's rapid pace of technology and multilateral and bilateral international trade agreements between countries have created endowments in some countries to manufacture products more efficiently. International contract manufacturing has enabled product innovators to design, redesign and develop their product ideas into a product using the manufacturer's design team at a fraction of the traditional product development process costs. International product manufacturers have created greater capacity to facilitate product design, development and contract manufacturing for their international partners. For example, today any entrepreneur is able to organise a trip to China to seek the assistance of a contract manufacturer to develop a product at a fraction of the cost compared to a similar product developed in Europe, America or Australia.

## Establishing a sustainable competitive advantage

To gain a competitive advantage in a market, the entrepreneur needs to create several core competencies to differentiate from competitors. For example, sourcing and importing products from international markets. This method will create a cost advantage and the company will become more competitive in its pricing strategy.

Product innovation creates uniqueness of your products in your market, and this will be more difficult for your competitors to match. Effective and consistent product innovation creates product differentiation and a greater competitive advantage that is sustainable.

Effective packaging and branding enable entrepreneurs to establish themselves more quickly. Strategic packaging associates your products with well-known brands, similarities in colour or design create cognitive resonance with consumers. Associate branding is another strategic positioning to establish and create trust for buyers to accept your product more easily. This strategy will enable a company to manage consumer dissonance.

## Selecting an effective selling method

There are hundreds of selling ways that a corporation can implement; nevertheless, Brian Tracy's psychology of selling is the most successful strategy to apply and sell right away. What's more, his relationship selling strategy works for the majority of people around the world.

In 2003, an Iranian corporation called Gold Quest began selling gold coins to the public through a pyramid scam, and the company grew at lightning speed. This corporation began in 2003 and continued until 2005, selling 800 million dollars' worth of gold coins without delivering a single coin to a buyer. This company used a Persian translation of Brian Tracy's sales psychology. That experience demonstrated that the connection marketing strategy works in all languages. The Iranian Government shut down Gold Quest in 2005 for scamming consumers. Nonetheless, the strategy had allowed the corporation to persuade customers to pay thousands of dollars without obtaining anything in return.

## Where to start

I am in no way encouraging anybody to even think about following the example of Gold Quest. And it is not necessary at all, to create a thriving innovation-based business. Every year, various international trade fairs are conducted in China, including the Guangzhou Canton Fair, which is one of the largest and most diverse product-based trade fairs in the world. Canton Fair is one of the best places to start your adventure of developing or sourcing new products.

The Chinese government has built significant capacity to facilitate endowment factors for Chinese firms to have easy access to financial services, human resources, and raw materials around the country. As a result, many factories have been created throughout China to suit the demands of foreign consumers. However, advanced manufacturing hubs have been established in several regions of China to cope with global brands that require high-quality products. For example, Fujian province is a hub for big running shoe manufacturers such as Adidas, while Jiangsu province produces the most efficient solar panels.

## Importing and products Sourcing

Sourcing from international markets requires effective and strategic supply management if a company is to remain competitive and profitable. For example, to source products from China, the importer must focus on quality rather than negotiating on price. Chinese factories and suppliers often offer low prices to international buyers.

However, new importers and international buyers often have a misconception about Chinese negotiation culture when dealing with Chinese suppliers. Inexperienced international buyers believe that they must negotiate for every product or service offered by Chinese suppliers in order to obtain lower prices.

In contrast, experienced international importers appreciate that Chinese suppliers often quote correct prices and that any further negotiation may result in the wrong product being delivered or may encourage the supplier to deliberately use inferior materials to produce inferior quality products to meet buyers' discounted orders. The international misconception of the price negotiation culture in China often results in inferior or sometimes unsellable products being delivered to international buyers.

International trade rules are complex and returning faulty products to international suppliers is difficult and unprofitable. For example, during my fourth trip to China in 2012, I placed an order to manufacture a folding handle for my blue Marblestone saucepan. My Chinese agent took control of our negotiations and asked the supplier for a further discount, so the supplier politely agreed to reduce the price by $800 from a total contract of $80,000.00 and took our deposit with a smile on his face. In addition, the agent's ego was boosted as he claimed to have saved on shipping costs.

However, the product was manufactured, packed and shipped to Australia on time. After we started selling the products, customers began to complain about the durability of the folding handle. During our initial investigation, we discovered that the supplier had changed the colour of a small locking device inside the handle that connects and holds the pot. This experience left us with no option but to redesign the entire handle, delaying our product release by a further six months.

## Purchase Terms and Conditions

To avoid such problems and import products efficiently, importers need to understand the following international trade terms and processes, including purchase term, pricing, payment and shipping terms.

## Purchase terms

International buyers must clearly state the terms and conditions that constitute an offer and how acceptance of the offer will be communicated. Identify the parties involved, such as buyer and supplier, with their legal names and contact details. Product or service descriptions must include product or service specifications, quantities, quality standards, packaging and delivery methods.

## Pricing terms

Pricing and payment terms must be clearly stated, including currency, unit price and any applicable taxes, duties or fees. Indicate accepted payment methods and terms, such as advance payment or deposit and balance payments. Any penalties for late payment or non-payment. Normal payment terms are 20-30% deposit and balance payments against Bill of Lading (BL), some suppliers also accept Letter of Credit (LC). International buyers can obtain a letter of credit from their banks.

## Delivery Terms

Specify the agreed delivery terms such as shipping method, delivery location and delivery times, including responsibility, packaging, labelling and insurance in transit. Define the inspection and acceptance process on delivery. Specify the quality control procedure and acceptance criteria by which the buyer can notify the seller of any defects or non-conformities.

## Intellectual property

Address the ownership and protection of intellectual property rights associated with the products or services purchased. Specify any licensing and use restrictions. Dispute resolution mechanisms such as mediation, arbitration and litigation must be specified, including jurisdiction and governing law. The need to include a confidentiality and non-disclosure clause in the agreement to protect buyers from competitors.

## International commercial trade terms (Incoterms)

Incoterms are a set of standardised trade terms published by the International Chamber of Commerce (ICC). They define the responsibilities of buyers and sellers in international trade transactions, including the allocation of costs and risks. Illustrations of Incoterms include Free on Board (FOB) and Cost Insurance and Freight (CIF) by supplier or

Ex Works (EXW), which means the supplier only charges for the product on the factory floor without any delivery costs.

## Import and export documentation

**1. Bill of Lading (BL):** A Bill of Lading is a document issued by a carrier or its agent that serves as a receipt for the goods being shipped and evidence of the contract of carriage. It includes details such as the description of the goods, the names and addresses of the shipper and consignee, and the terms of shipment.

**2. Commercial Invoice:** A Commercial Invoice is a document provided by the exporter to the importer, which itemises the goods being shipped, their value, and other relevant details. It is used for customs clearance and for calculating duties and taxes.

**3. Packing List:** A Packing List is a detailed inventory of the contents of a shipment. It includes information such as the quantity, description, and weight of each item, as well as the packaging type.

**4. Certificate of Origin:** A Certificate of Origin is a document that certifies the country in which the goods being exported were manufactured. It is used to determine the eligibility for preferential trade agreements and to assess customs duties.

**5. Import License:** An Import License is a document issued by the importing country's government that grants permission to import specific goods. Certain products or industries may require an import license to ensure compliance with regulations and to control imports.

**6. Customs Declaration:** A Customs Declaration, also known as an Entry or Import Entry, is a document submitted to the customs authorities of the importing country. It provides information about the imported goods, including their value, quantity, and classification for tariff purposes.

**7. Harmonised System (HS) Code:** The Harmonised System (HS) is an internationally standardised system for classifying traded products. Each product is assigned a unique HS code, which is used for customs purposes to determine the applicable duties and regulations.

**8. Letter of Credit (LC):** A Letter of Credit is a financial instrument issued by a bank on behalf of the buyer (importer), guaranteeing payment to the seller (exporter) upon the fulfillment of specified conditions. It provides security for both parties in an international transaction.

**9. Import Duty:** Import Duty, also referred to as customs duty or import tariffs, is a tax imposed by the importing country on imported goods. It is based on the value or quantity of the goods and serves to protect domestic industries and generate revenue for the government.

It's important to note that trade regulations and documentation requirements can vary by country and product. For instance, Australia custom requires packing declaration for all imports and fumigation certificate for some products. It is advisable to consult with trade professionals or customs authorities to ensure compliance with specific important export procedures.

In This chapter I have tried to cut to the chase and show you exactly how to create products and establish your competencies yourself, However, I will be available to assist you for product development, product sourcing, importing and products matching to your markets internationally. I also have sufficient experience and knowledge for setting up successful businesses and train you and your staff to become sales stars in your field. Furthermore, I invest in real estates, technologies and chicken farms. My expertise is available to be utilized around the globe with a small fee and your business will thrive. If you want to shortcut to achieve success in business then contact Hassan Varasi

On following emails: hassan1721@yahoo.com/info@Plusco.com.au

# Violet H. Mwandenga

Violet H. Mwandenga is a remarkable Life Coach who has dedicated her life to empowering immigrants, asylum seekers, and refugees around the world. Her own journey of resilience and transformation began when her husband kidnapped their three children from America to Africa, and she got them back after more than 2 years. This traumatic experience ignited her passion to bring hope to immigrants, help them find their inner strength and resilience and pursue their dreams, no matter what life throws things on them. With unwavering determination, Violet developed her unique coaching approach, Exposure Coaching, recognizing the unique challenges newcomers face in foreign countries. She believes that with the right tools, mindset, and support, anyone can excel in any market, regardless of their background. Her coaching is a beacon of hope, fostering aspiration and adaptability, while emphasizing the significance of a growth mindset and positive emotions.

SCAN ME

# Chapter 10

# UNLEASH BUSINESS BRILLIANCE: THRIVING AS NEWCOMERS

**Violet H. Mwandenga**

> **"The future belongs to those who believe in the beauty of their dreams."**
> Eleanor Roosevelt

In a world where borders blur, opportunities abound, and dreams know no bounds, the journey of immigrants, asylees and refugees stands as a testament to resilience, determination and the pursuit of success. "Unleash Business Brilliance: Thriving as Newcomers" is your roadmap to not just survive but thrive in the unfamiliar terrain of a new culture. In the following chapter, we will explore the essential strategies, mindsets and actions that can empower you to overcome challenges and achieve your business dreams no matter what obstacles you face.

## The Power of Your Journey

As an immigrant stepping into a new business and cultural environment, you are embarking on a path brimming with possibilities. While this journey may be filled with the unknown, remember that within you lies the courage to navigate these waters and the resilience to turn challenge into triumph.

Every immigrant's journey to a new life is filled with valuable lessons that can transform how you navigate your business and personal life. Your unique experiences provide you with a powerful perspective that is vital in the world of entrepreneurship. You have already successfully maneuvered through various cultures, languages and customs, acquiring valuable insights that can distinguish you in the business world.

The resilience you have demonstrated so far is a quality indispensable for entrepreneurship. Your capacity to see setbacks not as endpoints but as stepping stones to success shapes your journey. Winston Churchill's words, "Success is not final, failure is not fatal: It is the courage to continue that counts," reverberate with this experience.

## Align With Local Needs and Preferences

When starting a new business, it's crucial to be aware of your surroundings as you lay the foundation. Make sure to familiarize yourself with the business culture in your new environment. Conducting comprehensive market research will provide you with the necessary insights to customize your products or services to align with local needs and preferences.

Each market has its own distinct rhythm and set of guidelines. Achieving success involves adjusting your strategies to match the dynamics of the local market. Keep in mind that what was effective in your home country may need to be adapted in this potentially unfamiliar setting. This situation requires a mindset that is open to learning and able to adjust quickly.

Establishing a business always requires creating powerful partnerships and even more so when doing so in a new country. Look for mentors who can provide guidance, participate in business networks, and attend industry events to network with entrepreneurs who share your vision.

Make adaptability your trademark as you navigate the new business landscapes. The world's most influential thinkers encourage this; Tony Robbins claims: "Every problem is a gift. Without them, we wouldn't grow." In that sense, think of your business like a plant that grows – it needs the right environment, care and the ability to adapt to the seasons. With careful planning, a deep understanding of your new market, and a receptive mindset, your business will not just survive - it will flourish.

**Embrace a Growth Mindset**

Positive emotions and a growth mindset form the bedrock of success for any entrepreneur, especially those starting anew in a foreign country. These elements influence decision-making, inspire creative solutions to obstacles and usher in openness to various business strategies that could lead to outstanding results.

When you are away from home, dealing with the uncertainties of starting and running a business, keeping a positive emotional state is crucial. It helps you develop the resilience required to view challenges as chances for growth and learning, fueling your entrepreneurial drive.

Gratitude, mindfulness, and celebrating each accomplishment serve as tools to cultivate and reinforce positive emotions, ultimately setting the tone for how you experience your business journey. They help to build the psychological stamina necessary to persevere through demanding times.

Adopting a growth mindset means embracing the unknown with excitement, seeing setbacks as an incentive to innovate and appreciating the learning process inherent in entrepreneurship. It paves the way for persistent self-improvement and a dynamic response to the fast-paced changes of the modern business world.

Strategies to foster a growth mindset include:

- Actively seeking out learning opportunities
- Engaging with diverse perspectives
- Encouraging collaboration to enrich your entrepreneurial approach.

The goal is to create a forward momentum where intelligence and abilities consistently evolve in response to new experiences and information.

The quote from John F. Kennedy, "Leadership and learning are indispensable to each other," captures the essence perfectly. It underscores the interconnected nature of open-mindedness and the pursuit of knowledge—two integral components of a growth mindset.

**Entrepreneurship as a Land of Opportunity**

Entering the competitive world of entrepreneurship as a newcomer can be daunting, yet it also offers a land of opportunity. Entrepreneurship knows no borders; it's a universal playing field where your unique background can serve as a competitive edge. And while the journey of entrepreneurship is challenging, it does come with rewards; it pushes you to grow, adapt to new landscapes, and hone your business acumen. Through the shared wisdom and experiences of others, you can find the inspiration and guidance to forge your path, overcome obstacles and build your business with confidence.

Starting a business in a new country calls for courage, innovative thinking and a relentless drive to succeed. To give you the inspiration and comfort that success is within reach, get inspired by the countless stories of immigrant entrepreneurs who have turned their dreams into reality. From small start-up owners to leaders of thriving international companies, these trailblazers have paved the way with their persistence and ingenuity.

The key to these entrepreneurs' success lay in their ability to adapt: seeking out and embracing local cultures, needs and market trends. They exemplified how a deep understanding of the market, a well-crafted business plan and responsiveness to customer feedback can craft a business that resonates with people.

As you gear up to create or expand your own business, consider the importance of your personal brand. It's an expression of who you are and what you stand for, and it's as crucial for businesses as it is for individuals. Networking, showcasing your unique skills and experiences, and capitalizing on online platforms will help you build a compelling personal brand that speaks to your audience.

## Building Your Support Network

> *"Alone we can do so little; together we can do so much."*
> Helen Keller

In the world of business, the strength of your network can be as important as the quality of your product or service. For immigrant entrepreneurs, this is particularly true. A robust support system can offer guidance, create opportunities, and help you navigate the business culture in a new country.

Building a strong network starts with reaching out to local entrepreneurs, business leaders, and industry groups. These initial connections can open doors to mentorship, strategic partnerships, and deeper market insights.

Encourage engagement by being proactive. Attend local business events, join relevant groups, and participate in discussions. Every conversation is a chance to learn, and every interaction is an opportunity to make a lasting impression.

Develop your network by offering value and support to others. Volunteer your skills and expertise, connect others within your network, and be willing to lend a helping hand. A network is not a one-way street; it thrives on mutual benefit and reciprocity.

Technology has revolutionized networking by allowing us to connect with people around the globe virtually. Use social media, professional networking sites, and online forums to grow your circle beyond geographic boundaries. However, remember that online connections are most effective when they complement real-world relationships.

Finally, never underestimate the importance of maintaining the relationships you build. Regular communication, remembering details, and following up on conversations show that you value your contacts. This attention to nurturing relationships can transform casual connections into powerful allies.

**Leveraging Digital Tools for Global Reach**

The digital revolution has made it possible for businesses to connect with customers across continents with the click of a button.

A robust online presence starts with a user-friendly website, serving as your digital storefront. It's a platform to showcase your products or services, share your entrepreneurial journey, and build credibility. Design it to reflect your brand and to be accessible, providing a seamless experience for users worldwide.

Social media platforms offer a dynamic way to engage with your audience, understand their preferences, and respond swiftly to trends. Use these tools to craft a sincere and vibrant brand story, to connect personally with your customers, and to create content that resonates with different cultures.

Email marketing is another powerful tool to maintain contact with your clients, update them on new offerings, and provide valuable insights. It allows for personalized communication that can strengthen customer loyalty and encourage repeat business.

In addition to these, search engine optimization (SEO) enhances your visibility to potential customers. Investing in SEO means your business is more likely to be discovered by those searching for what you have to offer—a vital aspect of thriving in competitive markets.

Finally, e-commerce platforms can extend your reach, allowing you to sell to customers globally. They offer the infrastructure needed to handle transactions securely and to manage the logistics of shipping and delivery.

In this digital era, Anthony Robbins' words ring true for entrepreneurs: "Where focus goes, energy flows." Channel your energy into mastering digital tools to amplify your business. With dedication and strategic use of technology, your enterprise can illuminate the global market, serving clients far beyond borders.

## Compliance and Understanding Local Regulations

Engaging in business in a new country comes with crucial legal considerations. Knowledge of the local regulations is the non-negotiable groundwork for a long-lasting, reputable enterprise.

Access local resources, workshops or legal consultants that specialize in helping newcomers. They can offer a clearer picture of necessary documentation, tax obligations, employment laws, and any industry-specific regulations that apply to your business.

Simple mistakes in handling legal matters can lead to significant setbacks. Ensure proper handling of your contracts, business licenses, and intellectual property rights. Being meticulous in these areas demonstrates professionalism and integrity, traits that build trust with clients, suppliers and partners.

Stay up-to-date on any changes in legislation that may affect your business. Changes in regulatory landscapes are common and it's your responsibility as a business owner to keep abreast of these developments and adapt accordingly.

## Financial Mastery and Sustainability

Managing the financial aspects of a business can be one of the most complex yet critical challenges faced by entrepreneurs, particularly those operating in a new country.

Start with the basics: develop a clear understanding of cash flow, budgeting and cost management. These are the cornerstones of financial health for a business, allowing you to navigate through market fluctuations and economic changes.

Funding is another vital element. Explore local options for financing, which might include loans, grants, and investor funding. Each has its benefits and requirements, so thorough research and expert advice are key to making the right choice for your business.

Planning for the future is indispensable. Seek advice on long-term financial planning, including retirement accounts and investment strategies that align with your business goals. Sustainable growth comes from not only running the business effectively but planning for its future stability.

Be proactive about taxes. Understanding local tax laws can save your business a significant amount of money and prevent costly legal issues. Make use of professional accounting services or tax advisors who are well-versed in the intricacies of the local tax system.

Avoid the common pitfalls by educating yourself on the financial mistakes that entrepreneurs often make. This could involve underestimating costs, overestimating revenue or not having a financial safety net. Learning from others can help steer your business away from these errors.

In the words of John D. Rockefeller, "Do not be afraid to give up the good to go for the great." This is especially true in financial matters, where strategic risks and informed decisions can lead to greater rewards. Exercise caution, but don't shy away from opportunities that could lead to substantial growth.

## Your Secret Power: Adaptability and Persistence

In life and in business, the only constant is change; adaptability and persistence are the sails that allow immigrant entrepreneurs to navigate the winds of change effectively. Embracing these qualities unlocks the full potential of your entrepreneurial journey in a new country.

You have to be able to keep learning, come up with new ideas, and change your business plans as things change. "It is not the strongest of the species that survive, nor the smartest; it is the one most responsive to change," Darwin said about evolution. This is also true for entrepreneurs. If you want to stay ahead of the curve and find new growth possibilities, you need to be open to change.

Persistence is the force that keeps you going when things get hard. Churchill's wise words, "Success is not final, failure is not fatal: it is the courage to continue that counts," perfectly describe the attitude of an entrepreneur who doesn't give up. Failures and setbacks are unavoidable, but they can also teach you a lot and change the way you do things and your plan.

To cultivate these vital attributes, consider the following strategies:

- Leverage your unique experiences and perspective to bring innovative solutions to the market.
- Seek out constructive feedback and be willing to pivot your approach when necessary.
- Maintain clarity of vision but stay flexible in your methods to achieve your goals.
- Build discipline and resilience by setting incremental objectives and celebrating small victories.

**Your journey is Uniquely Yours**

Your entrepreneurial journey in a new country is filled with potential, rich with experiences that shape the way you view business and life. With readiness to confront challenges and heart to persevere, your path is that of brilliance waiting to unfold.

Your journey is uniquely yours, a reflection of bravery, perseverance and potential. Every action you have taken and will take adds to a beautiful journey of learning and development. Embrace the lessons from every failure and success, as they are crucial parts of the entrepreneurial journey.

But remember, entrepreneurship is not a solo venture. There are many individuals who share your drive and goals. Make connections, establish networks, and always keep learning. Every advice, every interaction contributes to your journey towards success.

As you look ahead, envision a future radiant with the promise of your achievements. It is there for the taking, for those who dare to dream and work tirelessly to turn those dreams into reality.

With this guide coming to a close, your real journey is just starting. Life can be full of uncertainties and challenges. With resilience in your heart and a clear vision in your mind, you will navigate this journey with wisdom and strength that transcends borders.

Visit www.ujlifecoach.com now and let the symphony of your success begin. The future belongs to those who dare to take the first step—make it count with Unique Journey Life Coach.

The world is waiting for your brilliance.

# Jeremy Howell

Jeremy Howell lives in a small town in the Jacksonville, FL area with his beautiful wife and family. He is currently a business coach, international speaker and a serial entrepreneur with a passion for helping business owners create freedom of time and money through his coaching practice Impact Value, LLC. He is an expert in Leadership development, delegation, and profit acceleration. He was inspired to become the best in all these areas because of the struggles he encountered in his early days of running an Assisted Living Facility. Jeremy found himself stressed out and overworked by this business that had become a prison. In order to break free, Jeremy began a journey of personal development and within a few short years gained freedom of time and money with the principles given in this book.

# Chapter 11

# TOO MANY HATS FOR ONE HEAD

**Jeremy Howell**

I'm often asked how I manage to travel the world and keep my business running while I'm away. My business is not only running, it is thriving. I hear so many business owners say they could never do this. It's the same people who complain about how they wish it was different. I will never tell you that my way is the only way, but I will tell you that it works. I can show entrepreneurs the way to freedom, but I can't make them take action. The key is to take action once you know it is possible and someone has shown you how. I know a lot of you are probably thinking, what do you mean by "take action"? All I do is take action! I know that 99% of small business owners definitely take action in their business. What I'm talking about is taking the right actions to create not only the business you want, but also the life you want. I also frequently hear the following statements (please let me know if any of those sound familiar):

This business can't run without me!

It won't get done right if I don't do it!

If you want something done right, you have to do it yourself.

These are the things we say when we are frustrated about not having proper delegation. Another reason could be that you're afraid to hire it out because you feel you can't afford to.

Let me ask you a question. When you started your business, did the vision of what you wanted match up with what you are currently doing? In other words, did you create the ideal life with this business? The answer for so many business owners is no. Why run a business if it doesn't create the lifestyle you want? If that's you, there's good news. You can change that. Most businesses here in the USA are small businesses, and they are the heartbeat of our country. Why is it that I own a business in the same industry as thousands of others, and I'm able to travel the world and live an entirely  different life than the owners two streets behind me? It's not the industry, it's the person running the business. If you are the CEO (Chief Everything Officer), then you are not going to be good and all the jobs and your business will suffer. The ability to put your ego aside and be completely honest with yourself is the beginning. Being able to admit that you can't be good at everything, but knowing that you can be great at one thing. That one thing has to be the creative development of your business.

Now there are many areas you need to develop if you are to create the freedom you have always wanted. I have divided them into these categories: Leadership, Systems, Delegation, Automation and Outsourcing. I want to explain that although I have a lifestyle I could only dream of in my earlier days, it's not because my business is passive. I don't think there are many truly passive ways to make a steady cash flow. I definitely play a role in my business, but it's only the roles that I'm great at and passionate about. I pay close attention to the heartbeat of my businesses and innovate in as many areas as possible to make that heartbeat as healthy as possible. In other words, I don't just set up the five categories and walk away. Each category has to be innovated and determined to be effective on a regular basis. That is what separates you from everyone else.

We are talking about SOPs (Standard Operating Procedures), not only to give you freedom, but also to remove chaos from the environment. Chaos in your organization will put off potential customers and employees, and they will go elsewhere. If you're an employee, and you don't have clear and concise job descriptions, or you don't have a good manager, it doesn't matter how much you're paid; you'll leave or be unhappy. You need to think like a customer and an employee, but act like a great leader with vision. A true visionary is really good at bringing the vision to life by articulating it to their team. Most of the time, when a business owner has a vision, they can see it clearly, but they lack the ability to paint a clear picture for those who will be responsible for implementing it. This is where the visionary (owner) gets discouraged and disconnected from his people. I'm going to go out on a limb here and say that your employees, for the most part, want to do a good job.

I hear many business owners make the following statements: These employees don't have what it takes these days. They say their employees are incompetent or even stupid idiots. That's a direct reflection on the management, not the employee. What kind of authority does the employee have over who stays and who goes? That's the manager's responsibility. So, if someone is not trainable or coachable, why are they in your organization? Take responsibility! Responsibility is the ability to react. You should respond as a great leader would. Respond in a way that cultivates what the employee already has. The employee has a desire to do a good job. We are programmed to want to fulfil our purpose in life. Not just some people, but all people want to be great at what they do. The people who don't work out either don't want to follow the leader or they don't have the desire to fulfil those duties. So, with that in mind, we will jump straight into leadership development.

Leadership Development is one of the most important things within a thriving business. Without great leaders, nobody knows whom to follow. The point of leadership is to not lead a whole bunch of followers, but to raise leaders in their department. As a leader, we must develop a vision and be able to articulate it clear enough so that everyone can share the same vision. If you don't know what you are aiming at, how in the world are you going to hit it? Many leaders are frustrated for this very reason. They have a clear vision but do not share it properly. They try to implement the vision, and they get upset with the ones that are supposed to be following because they don't have a clear aim. Once they have a clear direction, synergy starts to happen.

Leadership happens in every organization, but that does not mean that it's great leadership. If you have a high turnover rate or have plenty of complaints from employees or managers, it always stems from leadership. Most leaders in business have a disconnect with those who execute the vision. It's a 'my way or the highway' attitude. Or, stiff and inflexible, unwilling to compromise style of leadership that is a horrible way for any organization to reach success. This is what causes disgruntlement, bad attitudes and resentment towards the leader. Most people are naturally focused on the negative, so if they don't have a leader they respect, things go downhill. The first time something bad happens and that leader does not handle the situation properly, the negativity bubbles to the surface as soon as they walk away. The best leaders are able to draw out the problem-solving talent in their team. As a leader, you want your people to be able to think for themselves. The best phone call I can think of, good or bad, is when my team calls and says this is what happened and this is how we handled it. You see, as a leader, you want them to lead themselves. But they look to you for the overall vision.

As I write this, I am in Africa with my wife and business partner. Our manager contacted us via WhatsApp, which only works on Wi-Fi. She told us that one of our company cars had broken down 30 miles (ca. 48 km) from our office. I wasn't there to guide her through it, but she had the ability to make sound judgements that made me proud. It was very late in the day when I got back to my hotel room and read the news that I learned of this situation. At the same time, I learned that she had dealt with it in a similar way to what I would have done. That made me very proud of her! My wife and I slept well that night, knowing that our business was running and thriving without us. I have to give my manager the authority to think for herself. As long as she lands somewhere near the vision for my business, she needs to know that I will back her 100% every time. I had to share the vision properly to give her the confidence she needed to act without me, and that is how you gain respect as a leader. By allowing the people under you to use what God has already given them. He gave them a brain.

There are three reasons why people leave their jobs. Pay is the third reason. The number one reason is poor management. The second reason is that they feel that what they're doing doesn't matter. As a good leader, you have to understand that it's not just about being a good leader, it's also about meaning. No matter what the job is, it has to matter. All aspects of the job matter. If they don't know why it matters, or why it's important, then it won't matter to them. If you have any experience in the marketplace of working for different bosses, then you know the difference between a boss and a good manager. A boss will demand, and a leader will show and then relinquish authority so that you can meet their expectations. A boss will lose his cool when things don't go his way. A leader will find a way to make it a learning opportunity. It is not what happens, but how we react to what happens. If you react with anger, it does not feel good for you or the employee. If someone makes a mistake, you need to make it their idea to solve the problem and show you what they've learned from the situation. It is not the employee's responsibility to automatically know the right process, but it can be something that a manager pulls out of them. If you do it right, you should only have to do it once. From then on, the employee will not make the same mistake again. What happens is that bosses will say things to employees to put them down and ruin their confidence and self-esteem, or push them out of the way by saying, "That's not the way to do it!" Or "I'll just do it myself!" That's a good way to ruin someone's self-esteem. As a great leader, you want to do the opposite. You want to build their self-esteem, and you want them to hear your voice when certain situations arise, guiding them to do the right thing. As a leader, you should always look at every situation in two different ways. When things go your way, it is a blessing. When things don't go your way, it's a lesson. Blessings and lessons.

Teaching your staff this concept of blessings and lessons will trickle down to those below them and create a culture where it is not what happens, but how you react, that matters most. Leaders set the tone. Whether you're a boss, AKA a bad leader, or a leader, you set the tone. You're the model for how things are done. Like a child, they do what they see, not what they are told. Employees are the same, as soon as you walk away, whatever you said goes out the window. If everyone follows the leader, that means everyone is watching the leader. You've got to have integrity, and you've got to stay calm and in control of every situation. Even if you're scared to death. For example, during COVID-19, everyone who worked for us acted like the sky was falling. Stephanie, my wife, who was in charge, told our staff, who were visibly upset, "Nobody is allowed to freak out until they see me freak out first!" She set the tone for the staff and kept her composure because she understood that if she fell apart, so would everything else.

Only a small percentage of the people who work for you are not meant to work for you. As a manager, you have to be able to recognise when someone is not coachable and get rid of them quickly. My manager, Kristin, is relatively new in her position and I have been able to develop her into an excellent manager and leader. There is a difference between the two. If you can find someone who can do both, put them where they belong. She is now in a position to recruit. I used to be involved in the interview process, but I have now given her that responsibility. She knows the process and does it better than I do. That's the whole point of developing leaders. As a business owner, you want your business to run when you are not there. You have to do some work up front and develop the right leadership. You'll find that once you find the right person to coach, and they show you that they have the ability, they can and will often do it better than you. That is the first place to start, with leadership. Find classes, courses, seminars and require them to read certain books to continue their growth as leaders.

While leadership is the most important place to start to gain freedom and begin the process of letting your business run and grow without you, there are four other areas that you must focus on and develop to achieve this freedom. Delegation, Capture Systems, Automation and Outsourcing. These five areas will be covered in my book, which is currently in development.

# Scott Vaughn

Scott Vaughn is a seasoned entrepreneur with over 18 years of experience as a successful business owner and real estate mogul. Married for over 30 years and a father of three children, Scott understands the balancing act of family and owning multiple businesses day-to-day. Having successfully developed a multitude of retail stores as well as grown a real estate portfolio, he brings a wealth of experience to the table. As the founder of Wingo Coaching, Scott leverages his entrepreneurial journey to help business owners develop a winning mindset, create intentional marketing plans, and implement proven sales strategies. He loves partnering with business owners to help them crush their goals, relieve stress, and unlock time for their families.

SCAN ME

# Chapter 12

# HOW TO GET PEOPLE TO WANT TO BUY FROM YOU AND HOPEFULLY, ONLY YOU.

**Scott Vaughn**

When I first got into business, I didn't really know much about how to run a business, market it and make it profitable. As we continued to grow, I began to realize that the marketing we were doing was causing people to want to buy from us. Whether large, medium, or small, your business can use the tools we've learned to make people want to buy from you and hopefully, only you.

Your customer base likely has 1000s of choices on where to buy what you're selling. In this chapter, we're going to look at a few of the most important motivators that move people to choose a brand, a certain store or restaurant to spend their hard-earned money. These motivators are the formula for getting people to want to buy from you, and hopefully, only you!

## Inspire

The first thing is that your business must inspire them. This is foundational in motivating people to go to the trouble of going to your website, getting in their car with their money or credit card, walking through your door and purchasing something. Alternatively, if you're a web-based company, they're so inspired by your mission that they will forsake the thousands of other companies and put items in the cart and buy them because they WANT to buy from you and only you.

Nothing happens until they are inspired by something in your marketing, and we will look at some examples of companies that do just that. Why would someone pass by several other businesses or restaurants that are less busy to deal with the traffic at yours?

## Customer Experience

Back in 2000, I took on a new job and needed a truck. I had my orientation at the company, which was south of Atlanta, and at the end of the day, I decided to go truck shopping. I had done some research and decided to get the new Toyota Tundra that had come out that year. I went to a gas station, picked up the Atlanta Journal-Constitution, looked through the classifieds, and found an ad for a slightly used one at Stone Mountain Toyota, which is east of Atlanta. I called and got a salesperson, who told me to hurry because someone was looking at it. Fortunately, Atlanta has extraordinarily little traffic, especially late afternoon (that's a joke, by the way), and while I was on my way, the salesperson called and said the used Tundra sold, but he had a brand new one just like it and that he'd make me a good deal. I scurried up to Stone Mountain, and there it was, a brand new 2000 Toyota Tundra in Sunfire Red Pearl with all the options I wanted. He even had it cleaned up for me. The salesperson was an enthusiastic young fellow who made an immediate impression on me even before I met him. He knew what I wanted and had it prepared for me. We met, and he urged me to take it for a spin, which I couldn't wait to do, while the used car manager evaluated my trade in. We had a great conversation during the drive, and he was never pushy or too salesy to me. Critical point: NOBODY likes a pushy salesperson.

After some negotiating, I was about to drive away in my brand-new truck! It was after closing so they weren't able to do a thorough detail or fill it up with gas, so the salesperson found out when I'd be coming back through the next day to head home. When I arrived the next day, he had the detail department ready to go. He then took me out for a nice lunch and when we got back, the truck was stunningly clean. He then took me to the gas station, and I started to put regular gas in it, but he insisted on paying for premium fuel because "a beautiful truck like this deserves the best"! I drove home that day with a smile on my face so big, I could have eaten a banana sideways!

Everyone I met there had a phenomenally positive attitude and made me feel like the most important person in the world. Do you want to know what else it made me? It made me remember that terrific customer experience so much that I'm writing to you today about it in detail over 23 years later. So, I've got a question. What are you going to do today, delivering your own customer experience that will make someone so grateful that they would tell other people about it 23 years from now?

If you really want to double your income, you MUST deliver an experience that your customers/clients don't expect

## Marketing

What can we learn about marketing from the Stone Mountain story? It's not like newspapers are the way to go these days. Your website is yesterday's newspaper. Your website must be elite level because your prospects are going to search it before they ever think about buying from you. After having gone through a painstaking process of developing and redeveloping our company's website this last year, I can tell you that it won't be easy. However, it will be worth it because everyone, and I mean everyone, will look at it before they even think about buying from you. Another vital note is that it must be very user-friendly for a mobile device. At this point in history, everyone from 9 to 99 has a cell phone and if you'll notice that they're constantly looking at it regardless of where they are or what they're doing. It's sad really, but people are truly addicted to their phones. If you're going to double your productivity and income, your marketing and especially your web presence must be optimized to take advantage of this phenomenon.

## Eliminate the negatives

I used to referee college basketball and to get approved to officiate in different conferences, you have to go to summer camps. Later in my career, I went to a camp and ran into Larry Boucher, one of my first officiating mentors. We had known each other for many years, and he invited me to lunch. I was asking him about how to move up to some bigger and better conferences, and he had noticed I'd put on a few pounds and unfortunately, started to develop a bit of a dad bod. He looked me over, poked me in the belly and said, "you do a fantastic job and always have, but the first thing you need to do is to 'eliminate the negatives'".

I never forgot what he said and now in business, I utilize that advice more than I ever did in my officiating career. When you are in a competitive business environment, you must not only know what your negatives are, but also what your competitor's negatives are. When I was coaching basketball, we watched a lot of film of our upcoming competition. The best scouts, which I am not, are great at picking out the competitor's negatives to take advantage of them. In fact, my manager and I went to a new competitor in town to welcome them and to pick up anything about what they're good at and not good at. We scouted them and had a good idea of how we'll take advantage of their weaknesses. They, likewise, stopped in to do the same and hopefully, we didn't have any obvious weaknesses for them to take advantage of.

So obviously, you must not only scout your competitors, but also scout yourself. Give your business an honest look and write down your biggest weaknesses so that you don't give your competition a chance to take advantage of it. Moreover, have friends or colleagues check you out and give you honest feedback so that you can fix problems to improve your business. If you're not giving yourself an honest evaluation, then rest assured your competitors are, and they're definitely going to find the chinks in your armor and take full advantage of it. These issues are going to keep you from reaching your goals of doubling your productivity and income.

**Giving back**

Many years ago, I was leading a group of people through Dave Ramsey's Financial Peace University. The class was to help people manage their finances much more effectively and to get out of debt. I'll never forget the last lesson of that video session; Dave held out his hand with a wad full of cash and said that after you go through all the steps to get out of debt and build generational wealth, you must give back. He concluded by saying that if you build up wealth and your idea is to just keep it (he clinched his fist around the money), then you missed the point. You must be willing to give some of it back either to your church, a homeless shelter or whatever mission you want to accomplish with it.

I've taught my children throughout their upbringing that the best kind of giving is to give to someone you know has a need, doesn't even know you're giving it to them and couldn't repay you even if they knew. God has a special way of blessing you as a giver. I can't recommend giving enough in this way. The blessing far outweighs the cost, and you'll build a legacy of givers and make this world around you a much better place.

## Becoming the Greatest

In 2023, my wife, daughter and I went with some friends to Israel. The most memorable portion of the trip was a ride on the Sea of Galilee for lunch at Capernaum. Capernaum is known for a story in the Bible about a trip Jesus and the disciples took there. I'm not sure if they were on a boat, on foot or camel, but as the story goes, the disciples were arguing about who the greatest was among them. You've got to remember these guys were primarily fishermen or tax collectors, so they weren't exactly high up on the economic scale. In fact, they've never been known for anything of value in society. For them to be arguing about who the greatest is, is like the bench warmers on a football team having the same argument, when the fact of the matter is that none of them were good enough to be playing in the first place.

When they got to Capernaum, Jesus asked them what they were arguing about. They likely felt foolish telling their leader that they all thought they were the greatest, and Jesus' response is what I want you to gather here. He said, "whoever wants to be first, he shall be last of all and servant of all." Now, that's not what they wanted to hear, but it's the truth. It's the truth for them, and it's the truth for you and me. Our employees will see our servant leadership and WANT to work for you. They will be given the ultimate leadership program by you, their leader, not by what you say, but by what you do, how you treat them and especially how you serve them. In the same way, your customer base will also see and hear of your servanthood in the community, (community can be locally, nationally or internationally) and they will WANT to buy from you and hopefully, only you. People WANT to spend their hard-earned money with companies who are, in turn, going to serve them and others. It makes them feel good that they could help you financially in your endeavors, as if it's supporting a cause!

One example is a sock company called Bombas. They are an online sock company with a mission to serve homeless people by donating a pair of socks for every pair sold at retail to one of 3,500 community organizations. Their opening website has a picture of two runners with their motto – Run Far, Feel Good.

When you purchase socks from them, not only do you get to buy terrific socks that you need, you also are a contributing partner in putting socks on the feet of a homeless person. Now that makes me feel good about buying from them! I'll actually go out of my way to buy from them and only them when I need socks or if I'm giving socks to my children for Christmas, they're going to get Bombas socks. Now that's servant leadership with a mission everyone believes in and will look forward to joining.

Speaking of feet, back to the story of Jesus and His disciples, later on, Jesus gives us an example of true servant leadership when he got on His hands and knees and washed His disciples' feet. I'll remind you that the roads weren't paved, it's hot there, and they wore sandals. You mix all that, and you have disgusting, sweaty, dirty feet, and their leader knelt down and washed all 12 of their feet in a display of the kind of humility and servanthood that we need to display in our businesses. If you do, I can promise you the word will get out and people will want to buy from you! If you're a brick and mortar like I am, they will drive past many of your competitors with a smile on their face and cash in their hand to join your mission. If you're an e-commerce like Bombas, they will pay a premium just to help you because they are inspired by your mission.

We're in the mattress and furniture business and a colleague of mine, Chris Gamble, came up with a similar idea that we have since adopted. It's called the "Buy a Bed, Give a Bed" program. We simply give a bed to a local charity for a child who doesn't have one for every bed purchased. We consistently have people drive over an hour to buy from us so that they can in turn give a bed to a child in need. We originally implemented the program to help with a need in our community, but we've found that there are many outstanding people that want to join us in helping the most needy among us, and we're grateful to share in our mission!

Think about your business…who are you serving? Whose feet are you washing? Why would anyone be inspired by their experience with you enough to talk about it 23 years from now?

These are the motivators that work together to build an unstoppable company that can double your productivity and double your income!

As a service to help grow you or your company, we offer consulting, coaching, and scheduling speaking events. Contact information and website:

# German Walas

German Walas is an influential global entrepreneur and business development specialist with a dynamic portfolio spanning real estate, agriculture, and technology. As the visionary co-founder of Weston Plus and the founder of Kunarquen, he has pioneered developments that unite advancements across diverse geographical landscapes. His leadership has catalyzed the transformation of acres into coveted residential communities and innovative industrial parks, establishing Weston Plus as a hallmark of quality and innovation. Beyond the realms of construction, German has significantly contributed to agricultural development with Global World, championing sustainable food production through strategic funding and business transformation. His accomplishments include the development and management of over 450 real estate units, cultivation of 20,000 acres annually, and the strategic navigation of business environments to foster growth and profitability. With a commitment to excellence and a passion for creating lasting impact, German Walás stands at the forefront of entrepreneurial success, reshaping industries and enhancing communities worldwide.

SCAN ME

# Chapter 13

# SMART INVESTMENTS FOR A BRIGHTER FUTURE

**German Walas**

**"The only way to do great work is to love what you do. If you haven't found it yet, keep looking. Don't settle."**

Steve Jobs

I was born into a prosperous family in Argentina. My mother hails from a military background and works as a lawyer, while my father, initially not wealthy, is now one of the wealthiest individuals in Argentina as an entrepreneur.

I find myself sandwiched between my two siblings, and for a long time, I was considered the black sheep of the family.

During high school, when I wasn't strumming my guitar, I delved into software systems and had a keen interest in robotics. Whenever I needed funds for my robotics or systems projects, my father would request my assistance in pricing systems or providing services for his business.

I relished those moments; even in my younger years, I preferred spending school breaks on my father's farms rather than at the beach with friends. On the farm, my true passion emerged as I honed my mechanical, welding, and machine operation skills, which proved invaluable later on. I remember struggling to see over the tractor's dashboard when I first operated it, my small frame necessitating me to lean heavily on the clutch. These memories now bring me immense joy and serve as the foundation for my current role as an agricultural entrepreneur.

My father's chemical company was having major money problems when I was a senior in high school. He asked me to help out in the afternoons and then from 6 am to 5 p.m. The value of a college degree pales in comparison to the lessons gained throughout those five years.

A watershed moment in my life occurred during that time, when I saw my father's business collapse. I went out on my own and settled in a small hamlet in La Pampa, Argentina, with a degree in agriculture and marketing. My main concentration shifted to wheat and cow farming.

My partner, who is an architect and engineer from Italy, and I were married soon after. She was the one who pushed me into my first building project, and I ended up adopting the Italian philosophy of development and construction methods.

The years went by quickly, and by the time I reached my 40th birthday, I was living in the US. A few years earlier, I had witnessed the US mortgage crisis and jumped into the US property market. Since then, my company has expanded across the US and into South America. We operate farms, build developments, and manage RE properties. This has been possible because of what my father's experience has taught me. I may not have copied his way of doing business, but I have learned the right way to negotiate and work as a team.

To be successful as an entrepreneur, I have drawn on many different aspects of my life. Skills, education, and knowledge have been important. I have always worked hard. But the most critical skill I have learned is how to build teams. The team is the most important asset of my company. The team will take it to the top or can drag me down in a matter of seconds. To make my business successful, I have to make my team successful. And in order to achieve this, I need to become the leader of my team.

Finding or starting a business is easy; there are plenty of opportunities literally lying on the street. The same goes for capital. There are billions of dollars sitting in bank accounts, waiting for the right investment. The only requirement is to find a place of confidence and trust. A place where investors feel comfortable. Trust is what makes you great.

As a leader, I know that my best asset is my success. This is something my mother taught me as a child. I am what I am;

what you see is what I am. I love my life and the way I act. I don't like to show off; I live a simple life. I cook, I wash, and I keep my house in order. I take care of my children, and I love to spend precious time with my wife. We are in it for the long run. My family is my life, my home is my fortress. When night comes, I sleep well, without worries. And my heart is full of love. In the morning, I jump out of bed early, ready to dive into my passion. I say, let's do this!

Throughout my entrepreneurial career, I have seen others believe in me more than I believed in myself at the time. They saw skills in me that I did not see in myself. I think I matured as an entrepreneur when I finally started to trust myself. That was my 40th birthday.

The people around me trust me more, the more I work on my confidence, my vision, and my mission. When my team can see that in me, I can grow. Being a leader makes you excel in every aspect of your life, but you have to enjoy being there, or it won't last.

When you are searching for deals or negotiating, it is this trust in yourself that will get you to the finish line.

Being a team leader is a massive responsibility. As a leader, I like to push my team to try to beat me. I think that is the only way I can grow. If they can beat me, they can take my place. If I want to remain at the top, I have to continue to provide leadership, vision, and mission.

I have developed my vision by studying the context in which I am investing. I don't want to create something new. If I can study how to do something better, we will outperform the vision. My mission is to create businesses and make profits while having fun. I call myself a business artist. I enjoy every day at work; I enjoy finding solutions to my business problems, I love building teams and making them thrive. There is only one condition that any business I run must have. It has to let me have fun and enjoy myself.

Trust is the only thing that binds your business together. If they trust you, it is because you have earned it. The only way to earn trust is through time. Trust in your abilities, your vision, and your mission. Once your team sees you as a leader they can trust, you will have the company of people who will help your idea grow and flourish. Without my teams, I wouldn't have gotten to where I am today. The most important thing is to become the leader of the team, a leader your team can trust.

Trust is something I have to earn, and for me, that comes through my performance. And for that, I had to have a convincing vision, the right ideas that show them that they can trust me.

Yes, you have to teach your team, but also let them be the best version of themselves. They have to be free; they have to have their own voice. And I have to trust them, too. That relationship is what makes a business thrive. It is the work my team does that makes my business what it is today.

This year, I'm celebrating five decades in business. During that time, my company has not only survived, but thrived, making, financing, and operating investments in the US and South America. Over 160 million in total. It has been a journey of evolution, one in which I have taken on a leadership role and steered the course with a deep commitment to learning and sharing knowledge.

This journey not only shaped my professional development, but also fostered the creation of a cohesive team dedicated to realizing our collective vision. Together, we have embarked on a mission to promote exclusive projects and invest in companies that embody innovation and promise.

In the year 2020, Susan, a widowed mother of three teenagers, was coping with the profound loss of her husband, a respected surgeon who tragically succumbed to COVID-19. His death left a void in her life, both emotionally and financially. Faced with the daunting task of providing for her family alone, Susan recognized the need to invest her husband's capital wisely. In the midst of grief and uncertainty, she sought guidance.

An investment in our GW USA Fund II provided Susan with the financial stability she needed, allowing her to focus on helping her teenagers heal from their grief. Susan's investment exceeded her expectations, allowing her to live comfortably off the returns. She joyfully supported her oldest teenager's dream of attending college, a testament to her newfound financial security and unwavering commitment to her children's future.

The GW USA FUND II focused on an apartment building in Opa-locka, FL, that was nearly abandoned. The few remaining tenants were paying nominal rent, and the property was showing signs of neglect, with sections of the roof even missing. Originally inherited by a prominent Boca Raton attorney from his late mother, who lived there until her death, the heir lacked property management expertise.

The opportunity arose at the height of the COVID-19 lockdown, when uncertainty loomed over the financial markets and banks closed. Vigilance and risk management were key; failure was not an option. We seized the opportunity, recognizing the potential for transformation despite the crisis.

Although the pandemic did pose additional challenges, the construction team repaired the building quickly, using the opportunity to accelerate the process. At the same time, the office team meticulously curated a tenant roster that catalyzed the revitalization of the area. This strategic approach not only reinvigorated the property, but also caused neighboring property values to soar.

The success of our investment was underlined by the company's auditor, who praised our thoughtful risk management and decision-making, reaffirming our commitment to delivering exceptional returns for our investors.

Similar to GW USA Fund II, our GWA Fund IV represented a compelling opportunity in the real estate landscape. We capitalized on land acquired from debtors of a defunct financial institution and divided it into ten segments. We acquired each plot in turn, culminating in the creation of a vibrant 300,000 square meter development.

This ambitious project seamlessly integrated a range of amenities to meet a variety of needs and preferences. From a retail base and upscale restaurants to office complexes, a luxury hotel, a convention center, and medical facilities, the development offers a multi-faceted experience. It also offers penthouses and condominiums tailored for individuals, families and those going through life transitions such as divorce.

As the first phase nears completion, we are pleased to report returns that exceed initial projections, underscoring the success of our strategic vision and careful investment approach. This performance reinforces our commitment to delivering exceptional value and sustainable growth for our investors.

Maxi, a close friend and accomplished commercial pilot, played a key role in this investment. Our paths first crossed when I was studying to become a glider pilot, and Maxi's friendship has been invaluable ever since. While Maxi's career as a commercial pilot in Asia provided him with a comfortable income, he lacked the time, resources, and expertise to navigate the complexities of investing on his own.

Recognizing the mutual trust and respect between us, Maxi turned to me for guidance. He saw our fund as a solution to his dilemma, an opportunity to entrust his savings to a trusted ally, while he pursued his passion for flying. With reassurance and conviction, Maxi entrusted his financial future to our fund, knowing that his hard-earned savings would be carefully managed and grow over time.

Our partnership embodies the essence of collaboration and trust, where Maxi's dedication to his trade blends seamlessly with my commitment to thoughtful investment management. Together, we chart a course for financial prosperity that allows Maxi to focus on what he loves while his wealth grows steadily in the background.

My journey as an immigrant in the US has been a blend of perseverance and resilience, shaped by my unique character. Amidst the challenges and triumphs, I've learned valuable lessons. If asked to give advice, I'd emphasize being true to yourself, pursuing happiness, and cherishing family ties. Reflecting on my past, I'd tell my younger self to trust instinct, take risks, and have an unwavering belief in authenticity. These principles have led me to success, and I'd pass them on to my younger self with great confidence.

At Global World USA, we specialize in providing investment opportunities tailored to the needs of qualified investors. Many of our clients are looking to maximize their return on investment so they can focus on their careers or simply enjoy life to the fullest. Whether you're looking to passively grow your wealth or actively manage your investments, we offer personalized solutions to meet your financial goals.

Explore our offerings at www.globalworldusa.com or connect with me directly on LinkedIn at

https://www.linkedin.com/in/germanwalas/.

Let's take the road to financial prosperity together.

# Mauro Campagnaro

With a passion for financial mastery and entrepreneurial triumphs, Mauro Campagnaro embarked on a transformative journey from esteemed corporate roles to becoming a seasoned financial services advisor and coach. He found purpose in sharing advanced financial concepts, solving problems, and guiding entrepreneurs to unlock their full potential. Mauro draws wisdom from a courageous foray into entrepreneurship, navigating challenges and turning setbacks into opportunities. A visionary leader, he revitalized a consumer-packaged goods company, exemplifying a holistic approach to growth. Mauro is renowned for the 4-pillar strategy, fostering a growth mindset, optimizing tax and wealth, building powerhouse teams, and securing entrepreneurial continuity. Today, Mauro continues to empower entrepreneurs, envisioning a future of doubled productivity, income, and holistic success.

SCAN ME

# Chapter 14

# UNLOCKING FINANCIAL MASTERY

## Transforming Corporate Constraints into Entrepreneurial Triumphs and Doubling Productivity with the Strategic Influence of Financial Services Advisory

**Mauro Campagnaro**

> *"Every minute you spend in planning saves 10 minutes in execution; this gives you a 1,000 percent Return on Energy!"*
> Brian Tracy

After more than two decades of climbing the corporate ladder, I had reached a breaking point. Yet another pointless meeting left me feeling unfulfilled. I stared out the boardroom window and wondered, "Is this it?"

At that moment, I had an epiphany—why was I helping giant corporations make more money when I could be empowering passionate entrepreneurs? An insatiable hunger to share what I'd learned took hold.

I soon handed in my notice and decided to move into financial coaching. Now I guide experienced entrepreneurs through the pitfalls I once faced. My mission is to shorten their learning curve while sharing proven financial strategies.

The spark was my desire to give back by lighting the way, so others wouldn't stumble in the dark. Financial Mastery Coaching has allowed me to combine my corporate experience with my own entrepreneurial desire.

And how exactly do I empower entrepreneurs to unlock their potential? By equipping them to conquer three universal challenges:

First, strategic clarity. Seasoned entrepreneurs need a soundboard to pressure test ideas and gain insights. I provide that blend of mentorship, market know-how, and financial lens to help them evaluate opportunities rationally.

Second, executive bandwidth. Growth inevitably strains an entrepreneur's ability to manage everything effectively. I teach productivity hacks and provide training for delegating, streamlining, and accelerating.

Third, profit optimization. As enterprises scale, it takes financial savvy to maximize gains. My specialty is illustrating how small structure tweaks make a big tax difference, while advising on growth funding beyond traditional loans.

My method is personal. I start by intensely listening and understanding distinctive needs. Then, through a blend of business consulting, financial advisory, and coaching, I create customized strategies to drive breakthrough growth.

## Lessons Learned

Taking the plunge into entrepreneurship after two decades in respected multinationals within the consumer goods industry took considerable courage. In 2007, I ventured into the creation of a distribution company specifically tailored to the thriving natural products sector. Recognizing the upward trajectory of natural products, I took on the challenge with a determination to succeed. The first five years proved to be the most grueling as I navigated the demanding and soul-searching landscape of entrepreneurship. Starting a family during this time added an extra layer of complexity, but with a bold spirit, I was convinced that trying entrepreneurship was essential to avoid a lifetime of regrets. I firmly believed that failure was not an option; even if I faced setbacks, my age, and resilience would allow me to pivot.

My initial naivety became apparent as I embarked on countless 12- to 18-hour days, fueled by a financial cushion that sustained the business through its infancy. Eventually, I emerged on the other side of this climb, seeing the summit in the near distance. A dedicated team, particularly a steadfast executive assistant who had been with me since the second year, played a pivotal role in doubling sales within just 12 months. Sadly, despite this momentum, the cards were stacked too high and too thin to weather an unexpected shift. The personal toll was profound when my life partner, my wife, decided to part ways, marking the beginning of the end for my solo distribution venture.

However, as the saying goes, things happen for a reason. My current love reminds me of this constantly, and I give her credit for being right. Despite the ensuing challenges, I had enough resources to last another 18 months. An 'ah-ha moment' emerged from conversations, revealing the invaluable insight that talking to people can yield. My IT person, also connected to another company I encountered through an introduction, became my unexpected life vest.

This connection not only provided financial relief but set the stage for a transformative collaboration that had made our distribution company one of the most respected in Canada. The buzz around our success was palpable, a testament to how we turned the ship 180 degrees, doubling revenue and net income in four years. This journey, with its twists and turns, underscored the transformative nature of entrepreneurial resilience, ultimately reshaping my trajectory in profound and unforeseen ways.

**Proof of Concept**

Taking the helm of a consumer-packaged goods (CPG) company, I saw a crucial chance to apply my method for identifying problems and spurring growth. My first step in leadership was a deep dive into the existing challenges. I quickly pinpointed a major issue: our products weren't matching up with the latest consumer trends. Knowing how vital it is to stay relevant in a fast-changing market, I steered us towards a complete update of our product line, ensuring we were in step with what customers wanted.

But that wasn't all. I also spotted internal stumbling blocks. To tackle these, I rolled out strategic improvements in how we operated, making our processes leaner, which not only upped our efficiency but also cut down on costs. Part of this revamp meant better supply chain tactics and bringing in tech solutions to improve our overall productivity.

Understanding the power of customer engagement to drive growth, I drew from my experience in the natural products field to launch marketing initiatives that hit the mark with changing consumer trends. This strategy was deeply centered on the customer—it not only kept our current clients close but also drew in new ones, leading to a noticeable uptick in sales.

But I knew that to truly fuel growth, the team powering our efforts had to be onboard and energized. Recognizing the value of a driven, united workforce, I introduced specialized training programs and set up incentive structures to nurture a workplace where innovation thrives and everyone shares the same goals. The result? Happier employees and a significant rise in productivity, both of which are essential to a successful business.

Financial savvy was instrumental in steering the company towards a profitable course. I put strategic financial planning into play, smartly directing resources and narrowing our budget focus on areas that would give us the best return on investment. This shrewd approach didn't just stabilize our financials—it set us on a path of continuous profitability.

In the grand scheme, the turnaround story of the CPG company is a testament to a comprehensive strategy I used to pinpoint issues and spur growth. Tackling the internal roadblocks, realigning our product range with what customers were looking for, dialing up customer engagement, nurturing a team-driven environment, and plotting out financial strategies brought the company back to life. This all-around approach led to a striking bounce-back in both sales and profits over just a short period of time.

## My Four Pillars Model to Unlocking Your Entrepreneurial Potential

## 1. Growth Mindset Mentality

My experience with embracing a growth mindset isn't confined to my professional life; it's had a remarkable effect on personal relationships as well. A prime example is the transformative journey of my partner's son, whom I guided using the principles of the growth mindset.

I began by reframing obstacles as opportunities, highlighting that setbacks are not the end but rather the building blocks of success. This perspective shift is fundamental in developing a growth mindset.

I also introduced him to the idea of lifelong learning and remaining inquisitive, instilling in him the notion that errors are not dead ends but opportunities to learn and become more adept.

Resilience was another key area I focused on, underscoring the need to press on despite difficulties. This helps in overcoming the current challenges and builds strength for future hurdles.

Finally, I instilled the importance of positive affirmations and visualization. These techniques are powerful in fostering self-confidence and the belief in one's ability to achieve their goals.

These tactics collectively contributed to a profound transformation, nurturing a growth mindset that has positively influenced his academic and personal pursuits.

## 2. Leveraging Insurance and Tax-Friendly Investment Strategies for Financial Success

Understanding the complexities of taxes and wealth management, I've observed how strategic planning can create significant positive change for entrepreneurs, especially through the clever use of insurance products for tax-free investing. A standout tactic is the use of permanent life insurance policies. These policies are dual-purpose, offering a death benefit while building cash value that grows over time. Entrepreneurs can tap into this cash value with little or no tax penalties, depending on the situation, making it an excellent resource for their financial needs.

Moreover, integrating tax-friendly retirement accounts, like those coupled with a cash value life insurance policy, equips entrepreneurs with an income source during retirement that, in most cases, isn't taxed. But the role of strategic planning doesn't end there. It's also about astute tax planning techniques, seeking investment opportunities that resonate with long-term financial aspirations, and putting in place mechanisms that bolster wealth growth and safeguard it from potential risks.

Certainly, an additional tax-friendly approach stems from leveraging controlled debt instruments in banking. As an entrepreneur, my mantra emphasizes the paramount importance of ownership and views cash as the ultimate "king." This perspective underscores the significance of controlling and strategically managing debt, including decisions on repayment, payment structures, and interest terms.

This approach aligns with my broader commitment to empowering entrepreneurs with advanced financial concepts, offering them a comprehensive toolkit for sustained growth. By implementing tax-friendly investment strategies, entrepreneurs can optimize their wealth accumulation and shield their assets from unnecessary tax burdens, paving the way for a financially prosperous future. In essence, my insights illuminate the transformative potential of tax-conscious financial planning, providing entrepreneurs with a roadmap to navigate the intricate landscape of taxes and investments successfully.

Numerous entrepreneurs I engage with often find themselves wholly immersed in their businesses, losing sight of the initial aspirations that led them to embark on this journey. It's a common desire for entrepreneurs to envision their businesses flourishing to a point where they can comfortably retire. However, what typically eludes many is the practicality of systematically extracting returns from the business, multiples of the initial investments made. There is a misconception that the business alone can serve as a retirement fund. Unfortunately, this assumption can be detrimental, leaving entrepreneurs perplexed as to why, despite years of dedicated effort, they have so little personal gain to show for the substantial investment in building their businesses. It underscores the importance of adopting a more strategic and nuanced approach to ensure that the fruits of entrepreneurial labor translate into tangible personal wealth and a secure retirement.

### 3. Building a Powerhouse Team

For entrepreneurs aiming for comprehensive support, assembling a robust team of advisors is essential. Based on my experience, there are four key professionals that are critical for a successful entrepreneur's support system.

First is a knowledgeable financial advisor, who plays a pivotal role in managing wealth and crafting investment strategies. This expert works closely with entrepreneurs to ensure that financial plans go hand-in-hand with their business aspirations, aiming for peak financial performance. This person plays the pivotal role as the "quarterback," figuratively speaking.

Next is a competent accountant, whose expertise is invaluable. They're in charge of maintaining financial records, keeping things aligned with tax laws, and delivering strategic tax advice.

The third essential player is legal counsel. They're the guardians of the legal side of the business, navigating everything from contract talks to staying in line with regulations. Furthermore, ensuring a well-designed corporate structure is in place to properly capitalize on the strategic plan and financial instruments the financial advisor recommends.

Lastly, a seasoned business mentor or coach is crucial. They offer wisdom and different viewpoints that are key for strategic decisions and personal growth.

In my interactions with business owners, I've noticed that the absence of these advisors often leads to gaps in support, potentially derailing their success. For instance, not having legal counsel might leave the business vulnerable to legal hurdles, while the lack of a financial advisor could mean wealth isn't managed as effectively as it could be. Money could be left on the table and some taxes mitigated. And without the sharp insight of an accountant, maintaining financial records and complying with tax requirements could become a challenge.

## 4. Legacy and Succession Planning

For entrepreneurs, establishing a durable legacy and ensuring the seamless handoff of their life's work is crucial. Drawing on my own professional experiences, I'm a firm believer in the proactive adoption of strategies that can pave the way for a worry-free future.

One key strategy is the development of an exhaustive estate plan, which not only lays out how assets will be distributed, but also tackles the potential tax consequences. Such forward planning doesn't just ease the transition of wealth; it also helps avoid disputes among those who stand to inherit.

But it doesn't stop there. Setting up a governance framework for the family business is another step that can make a big difference, creating clear guidelines for future decision-makers and keeping business operations steady even in times of change. Utilizing trusts is another smart move, securing assets for the entrepreneur's descendants while providing financial stability through the generations.

Incorporating these pivotal elements early in their entrepreneurial strategy empowers business owners to take charge of their legacy, guaranteeing sustained success and smooth handovers for years to come.

## How you can turn your vision into reality

> *"If you want to be successful, find someone who has achieved the results you want and copy what they do and you'll achieve the same results."*
> **Tony Robbins**

Imagine a future where entrepreneurs soar beyond financial gain and experience a profound transformation that enhances every aspect of their well-being. My four-pillar approach is designed to make this vision a reality. This strategy is designed to unlock the extreme potential of entrepreneurs by creating a mindset that values growth in all its forms, not just on bank statements.

With this attitude of constant evolution and continuous improvement, entrepreneurs can tackle every obstacle with grit and see every setback as an opportunity. It's a mindset that promises more than a thicker wallet—it's about living a life of satisfaction and leaving a legacy that lasts.

By embracing my methods, entrepreneurs can set their sights on a future where they can double what they achieve and earn, paving the way not just to financial independence, but to a life that is richly rewarding and deeply meaningful.

Consider the story of an entrepreneur whose business had plateaued, his progress hampered by self-doubt and difficulties with taxes. By applying my four-pillar approach, an extraordinary transformation unfolds. First, a shift to a growth mindset sparks creativity and a renewed sense of drive. Next, they adopt strategic financial practices, such as using tax-exempt insurance investments, which turbocharge their financial trajectory.

The third strategic move is to build a robust support team—financial gurus, accounting pros and legal aces—that covers all the bases of entrepreneurial support. And the capstone? A carefully crafted legacy and succession plan that solidifies the future of their business and its lasting impact. This example vividly illustrates how the 4-pillar approach can transform entrepreneurial roadblocks into launch pads for success that reach new heights.

This is where I come in: I'm here to help entrepreneurs take bold steps into their future with a wide range of customized services. My one-on-one coaching and mentoring helps them develop a mindset that's ready to grow, push the boundaries, and visualize a future where they achieve double the success and income. I also provide practical workshops and essential materials focused on tax management and wealth building, so they have the financial savvy to tackle the complexities of the business world.

But it's not all solo work; I connect entrepreneurs with a network of experienced professionals—from financial planners and accountants to legal advisors and business coaches—to make sure they have a world-class team behind them. I also provide insight and the right tools for legacy planning and passing the torch, ensuring they make a lasting impact on their businesses and communities.

With this full suite of support, entrepreneurs can confidently move toward their dreams, armed with the know-how and strategies to double what they achieve and earn, all while building a fully successful and fulfilling life.

 Don't wait — Connect with me now to start your journey so you don't miss out on what savvy entrepreneurs like you are missing out on.

# Afshin Sajedi

Afshin Sajedi is a Persian-British entrepreneur, luxury travel expert and an investor in real estate who has made a name for himself in the world of travel and marketing. Afshin is the founder and CEO of Jets 100, a leading name in the luxury travel industry since 1996. Under his leadership, Jets 100 has carved a niche in offering shared private jet experiences tailor-made for prestigious events like the Formula One Grand Prix and other international gatherings. Serving a global clientele that includes individuals and high-ranking executives, Jets 100 has become synonymous with luxury and exclusivity. With an eye on the burgeoning potential of South Florida, Afshin is actively seeking collaborations with distinguished leaders to elevate their travel operations, ensuring an unparalleled luxury travel experience. He has visited over 50 countries, journeying to each at least three times. This extensive travel has enabled him to personally vet numerous luxury hotels and resorts, ensuring that only the finest are recommended to his clients.

# Chapter 15

# BEYOND FIRST CLASS: REDEFINING LUXURY TRAVEL IN THE 21$^{ST}$CENTURY

## Afshin Sajedi

> *"We believe that life's true treasures lie in shared experiences, and our goal is to create moments that will warm your heart for a lifetime."*

Afshin Sajedi

The flight attendant closed the overhead locker with a warm smile. I returned the smile, even though I wasn't in the mood. I felt exasperated. Just a few minutes earlier, the flight attendant had informed me that there was no space left for my bag in the overhead compartment. She proceeded to bring it along with her to a location towards the rear of the plane.

This was not supposed to happen. After all, this was business class, and I had spent more than $5000 on the ticket. But the cost of my ticket wasn't the only issue that frustrated me. Due to having to deal with a very crowded airport, long lines to check my luggage, and a hold-up at the security line, in addition to a long walk to the terminal and gate, I had ended up arriving a bit late to my seat. Mind you, I was still on time, but a first-class passenger had arrived before me and used my overhead bin to store his additional bag. Paying for a business class seat was supposed to guarantee overhead luggage space above my seat, which was clearly not the case. And the flight attendant did not really try to help me, either.

To make matters worse, at the end of that flight, the aforementioned first-class passenger approached me. He opened the overhead compartment and retrieved his bag with an apologetic smile, leaving me still waiting for mine. This made me think back to another instance, where an expensive ticket—in that case for first class—had led to me having to wait for my luggage at baggage claim for over an hour. And to those times when my first-class flights were delayed or cancelled altogether.

There clearly was a gap between service promises and actual experiences with commercial airlines, highlighting the need for immediate change, or even better, an entirely new approach.

An idea took shape in my mind.

## Passion for Luxury Travel

But let's get back to how it all began.

I embarked on my career journey right after finishing college when I took a job as a customer service agent at the local airport in my hometown in Iran. I spent three years there, during which I also participated in numerous trainings and courses with the tourism board. This was a crucial period that prepared me for my transition into becoming a tour guide and later a travel agent.

Always driven by ambition and a desire for growth, I made a bold move to Dubai. And my travels didn't stop there; I journeyed across Asia, the Middle East, and Europe, before finally settling down in the UK in 2003. Over the next two decades in the UK, I gained extensive experience working with significant travel agents and tour operators, culminating in my purchase of a travel franchise in 2014. However, it was the challenges I faced while collaborating with suppliers and operators that drove me to realize my own vision for a travel brand, leading to the inception of my company Holiday Luxury in 2016.

At the same time, however, there was a noticeable disillusionment with traditional luxury: Even though I was successful in the traditional luxury travel market, I became increasingly aware of the industry's shortcomings. The frustrations that are inherent in public transit could not be eliminated by even first-class travel. After all, even the most expensive seats were in the same planes, subject to flight delays and even cancellations. As I came to understand, genuine luxury required going beyond the comforts of worldly possessions.

My customers at "Holiday Luxury" clearly expressed a desire for Authenticity and Connection. Like me, they craved a deeper level of travel experiences. They valued genuine connections with locals, off-the-beaten-path discoveries, and the feeling of being immersed in a destination, not just a tourist passing through.

In my eyes, personalization was the pinnacle of luxury. I understood that one-size-fits-all approaches regularly failed to satisfy discerning travelers. My own bespoke brand was founded on the belief that true luxury lay in tailoring journeys to an individual's unique desires and preferences.

I began to focus on control and freedom. The incident on the business class flight highlighted my desire to empower travelers. I wanted my clients to feel a sense of control over their itineraries, unburdened by the restrictions of traditional travel.

## "We take care of everything"

And I remembered an occasion, where I had booked a private jet (instead of a commercial airline) to fly from Ibiza to London. On my way to the airport, I received a text message.

"Dear Afshin, if you have a bag, please, could you arrive within an hour?" the text said. And then it went on:

"If you don't have a bag, 45 minutes is perfect. And if you get stuck in traffic, could you just send us a text?

We take care of everything."

It was not the first time I had booked a private jet. But at that moment, the conversation brought home the stark difference between the ease and comfort of private luxury air travel and even the most luxurious version of commercial airline offers. But I also knew that the difference in price would not make the former accessible to most people. The price tag was just too hefty.

## An idea was born

Nonetheless, I dove into extensive research, taking advantage of my excellent networks and connections into the travel industry. I noted that one of the prominent players offered experiences with private jets for large groups, typically serving an ultra-wealthy demographic with itineraries ranging from 13 days to five weeks, which came with very high costs. These experiences catered to billionaires and retired multimillionaires, positioning them as a role model for my own venture.

My research identified a gap in the private aviation market for entrepreneurs and C-level executives who were happy with domestic private jet travel but faced a dilemma when considering international or long-haul trips due to the prohibitive cost of chartering a private jet. Instead of paying for expensive charters, these travelers would downgrade their standards to commercial flights, which led to various inconveniences and a lessened travel experience.

My personalized experience of receiving a flexible and considerate service while flying private – being able to arrive 15–30 minutes before my flight's departure and the ability to communicate directly with the service in case of delays – was in sharp contrast to the impersonal and inconvenient nature of commercial flights, where travelers are typically asked to arrive at the airport several hours before their flight.

I came across countless related stories of inconveniences faced by travelers on commercial flights, such as lack of space for luggage, technical delays, and long waits for baggage, even when flying in premium classes like business class, again matching my own experiences. These reports highlighted the disparity between private and commercial travel and helped me shape my own customized model, which finally led to the foundation of "Jets 100" as a part of Holiday Luxury Corporation, providing a solution that combines the exclusivity of private jets with cost-effectiveness for long-distance travel.

## Shared private jet experiences

My secret ingredient was a flight share membership model, which enables members to enjoy the exclusivity of flying private without bearing the full cost of chartering a jet. By pooling together like-minded individuals that are part of smaller groups (between 13 and 19 individuals, including flight attendants), the service provides access to luxurious, curated travel experiences and also fosters networking opportunities.

As a starting point, I focused on locations and events revolving around Formula 1 (F1), a purely strategic decision. It's one of the highest-profile sports events that takes place across 24 worldwide destinations known for their popularity and the diverse reasons people travel there, such as business, leisure, or sports entertainment. "Jets 100" has chosen F1 as a touchpoint because of its global appeal and the profile of the audiences it attracts, which aligns with the clientele of luxury jet travel.

Currently, "Jets 100" offers departure points from seven cities: Miami, New York, Los Angeles, Dubai, London, Monaco, and Madrid, to over 24 different destinations. In addition to F1, we offer an experience to the Olympics in Paris and exclusive leisure experiences such as private island retreats. We are expanding to include additional illustrious events such as golf tournaments, tennis tournaments, polo matches, the Super Bowl, award shows like the Grammys and the Oscars, wine tours, global Fashion Weeks, and more. This expansion reflects a commitment to covering a wide range of international events that appeal to their clients, marrying private jet travel with the world's most exclusive occasions.

## My Guiding Principles

Whether at Holiday Luxury or later at "Jets 100", I am convinced that the following guiding principles, which I have adopted over my many years in the travel industry, are the real reason for the success of my companies:

**Time as the Ultimate Luxury:** I truly understand the time constraints these individuals face. My focus on bespoke itineraries means eliminating wasted time with unnecessary transfers, layovers, and inflexible schedules.

**Hyper-Personalization:** Private jets are already personalized to a degree, but I take it even further. I delve into clients' interests and preferences, creating experiences specifically tailored to their passions, be it private art tours, exclusive culinary adventures, company trips, employee incentive trips, or access to unique business events.

**Flexibility and Control:** My model allows executives and entrepreneurs to dictate the pace of their travel. Whether that means last-minute adjustments, spontaneous extensions, or integrating work needs seamlessly into the journey, they gain a level of control impossible with traditional travel.

**Beyond Point A to Point B:** My vision elevates the private jet from mere transportation into a tool for networking, cultural immersion, and personal enrichment – all tailored to the specific needs of the busy executive.

**Stress Reduction:** By meticulously handling every detail, my company minimizes the logistical and mental burden of travel. This allows my clients to focus fully on their business goals or relaxation, arriving refreshed and ready.

**Key Takeaways**

I appreciate that not all readers have a need – or interest – for luxury air travel, but I still think there are elements in my strategy, which would also be beneficial for you, regardless of what industry you are active in.

**Personalization is Paramount:** My story highlights the importance of personalizing customer experiences. The simple act of a text message providing flexibility in travel arrangements was a standout moment for me, emphasizing the value of personalized communication over generic interaction. This is a practice that can be transferred to any customer-facing business to enhance customer satisfaction and loyalty.

**Identify and Solve a Specific Pain Point:** I recognized the inconveniences of commercial air travel early on and saw an opportunity to solve this problem for a specific market segment. Other entrepreneurs and businesses can similarly find success by identifying a clear pain point in their industry and offering a targeted solution.

**Leverage Experience to Innovate:** With my deep background in the travel industry, I used this experience to innovate within the private jet space. My past work with various travel services provided me with the insights needed to create a new model for luxury travel. In any field, a strong foundation of industry knowledge can be the springboard for innovation. If you only take away one thing, it should be to become a true expert in your segment, and combine success criteria within that segment to come up with a truly innovative approach.

**The Power of Shared Economy:** My business model of shared private jet experiences is a testament to the shared economy's potential to disrupt traditional business models. By allowing more people to access a service typically reserved for the ultra-wealthy, I broadened this market and created a new niche. Are there areas where you can do something similar in your industry?

**Quality and Exclusivity Can Coexist with Affordability:** "Jets 100" challenges the notion that high quality and exclusivity must come with a high price tag. My approach demonstrates that it is possible to offer a premium service at a more accessible price point, expanding the customer base while maintaining high standards. I am challenging you to do the math in your niche. Which buttons can you press to make your services more affordable, without compromising on quality?

**Creating an End-to-End Experience:** Beyond the core service of private jet travel, both of my companies curate a complete luxury experience. This approach of offering a comprehensive solution rather than a single service can be applied across various sectors to differentiate from competitors. In today's world of over-specializations, being a full-service provider can actually be your USP (Unique Selling Proposition).

**Networking and Community Building:** The concept of connecting like-minded individuals through shared experiences is a powerful tool for building community. This can be a valuable strategy for any business looking to create a loyal customer base and foster brand ambassadors.

Adaptability and Response to Feedback: Throughout my career, I have shown the ability to adapt my business models in response to customer feedback and changing market conditions. This adaptability is crucial for businesses to remain relevant and competitive. In my view, this is actually a non-negotiable for any business, regardless of which industry they are active in.

### Conclusion: The "Jets 100" Difference

My philosophy in business is deeply rooted in the belief that luxury travel should not only be exclusive but accessible, bridging the gap between dreams and reality. With every step, my aim has been to use my deep-rooted passion and expertise in luxury travel to bring forth unique, collective experiences that redefine the essence of high-end journeys. The core of my proposition lies in crafting personalized, unforgettable travel experiences, making the seemingly unreachable dream of luxury travel a tangible reality for a broader community. Through innovative approaches like the "Shared" Private Jet Luxury Travel Experiences, I strive to democratize luxury travel, emphasizing the power of collective effort and shared dreams.

I'd like to conclude by sharing a compelling insight that resonated deeply with me. A survey was conducted with 100 millionaires who were at the final stage of their lives. They were asked, "If there's one thing you could do all over again in your life, what would that be?" Surprisingly, none of their answers had anything to do with their financial wealth. Instead, 100% of them expressed a common sentiment— they wished they had invested more time in sharing quality experiences and creating cherished memories with their loved ones. As they neared the end of their lives, all they were left with were memories.

If this has sparked your interest, I'd be delighted to hear from you. Please reach out via email at Support@Jets100. com or give us a call at +1754-799-2350. As a token of our appreciation, we're offering all readers of this book a complimentary 3-month Jets 100 membership. Let's embark on a journey of creating unforgettable memories together.

# Andre Abouzeid

André Abouzeid is an accomplished Canadian Czech entrepreneur, actively ivolved in the direct sales industry for over two decades. He currently resides in Dubai, United Arab Emirates.

André began his career in the hospitality industry in 1993 and then worked as a courier in 1998. Since 2000, he has worked up to become a leading figure in direct sales, real estate investment, and entrepreneurship.

In addition to his successful career, André has authored two books, "Street Smart Network Building," recognized as valuable resources for aspiring entrepreneurs. His books provide insights into the business world and helpful tips for building a successful network.

With a network that spans 65 countries, André has a wealth of experience in entrepreneurship. He has conducted numerous workshops and seminars worldwide, sharing his vast knowledge and experiences with individuals looking to unlock their full potential.

# Chapter 16

# HOW TO BUILD YOUR LEVERAGED INCOME BUSINESS IN 90 DAYS

**Andre Abouzeid**

> **"I would rather earn 1% off 100 people's efforts than 100% off my efforts."**
> John D. Rockefeller.

Picture yourself lounging on a sunny beach while on vacation. Then, your phone buzzes gently. It's not a work call needing your urgent attention, but a weekly payment coming in. This money isn't from working right now; it's from work you did in the past. You helped some people out a while back, and now they're making money for you. That's leveraged income—earning without constantly working directly. But there's a bigger picture to consider. Let's look at how to make your money work for you and build lasting wealth.

Leveraged income involves repeatedly earning from work done once. For instance, authors earn royalties each time their books are sold, while musicians generate income from past recordings.

Passive income, on the other hand, stems from investments or assets. It's making your money work for you through interest from savings, rental income, stock dividends, or business investments. While passive income often requires initial substantial capital, leveraged income is accessible to anyone willing to work, regardless of background. It relies on hard work and has the potential to create a lasting legacy for ambitious individuals. Therefore, our focus will be on leveraging income that anyone can pursue.

Why is it risky to depend solely on one income source?

In today's dynamic world, unforeseen circumstances like rising living expenses and job instability are ordinary. Technological advancements and global changes are reshaping industries, with automation replacing human labor. Consequently, job losses and business closures are prevalent, posing significant economic challenges.

Starting a new business now requires a more innovative approach. It demands significant time and money and entails risks. While many work diligently for money, aiming for financial independence and ownership of one's career or business is essential.

However, leveraging income presents new opportunities, especially in uncertain times. It allows you to earn repeatedly from work done once, providing stability, freedom, and opportunities for success in a changing landscape. You don't need to invest vast sums of money.

Now, let's explore the steps and opportunities available in the marketplace that can help you achieve leverage within 90 days.

**1. Cultivate the Right Mindset:** Many of us have been conditioned to follow a conventional path: go to school, get good grades, find a secure job, or start a small business. My parents, both doctors, followed this route until they realized its limitations. Despite their hard work and dedication, their business ended with retirement because they lacked leverage and passive income. It's crucial to break free from society's programming and self-limiting beliefs. Understand the power of leverage and recognize the subconscious influences that may hold you back. Many individuals have started without money, connections, or academic qualifications, yet they succeeded through the right strategies. You can do the same by embracing the mindset of possibility and resilience.

> *"Entrepreneurship is more than a business; it's a mindset, a way of life, and a force that drives us to dream big and take bold steps."*
> Joseph Bismark

**2. Identify Your WHYs:** What motivates you to seek extra sources of income? It could be wanting to be financially free, supporting your family, or finding meaning in your work. Figuring out your reasons is critical because you need to know why you're doing something to understand how to do it. For example, I hated my job because I always struggled with money and wanted to support my family while living more meaningfully. Knowing your why helps you set clear goals and find the right path.

**3. Stay hungry, stay humble:** Begin with the 'I am broke' mindset. Invest in daily learning and growth. Avoid relying solely on the money in your bank account or past successes. To maintain productivity, I continuously invest my earned income in personal development, my business, and assets that generate passive income. Break free from your comfort zone.

> *"The comfort zone is temporary, illusionary, and completely redundant."*
> Vijay Eswaran.

**4. Set Clear Financial Goals:** Know exactly how much money you want to earn and when you want to earn it. Think big and set ambitious targets. For example, aim to boost your income significantly, like turning your yearly earnings into monthly income. Ask yourself, is this my financial goal?

In my journey, I aimed to surpass $20,000, inspired by someone in my field who made it weekly. I believed that if they could do it, so could I. I set a three-year deadline for my first million through a home-based business, knowing it's even more achievable today.

Consider the sacrifices you will make over the next 3 to 5 years to reach your financial target. Be specific and careful in your planning. For instance, when I started, I gave up social outings and TV time and even reduced my sleep to 4 hours daily. Remember, delayed gratification is crucial at this stage.

Break down your financial target into a clear plan by reverse-engineering your first income goal. For example, let's break down earning $200,000 a year into smaller steps:

Annual Income Goal: $200,000

Monthly Income Target: $200,000 / 12 months = $16,667 per month

Weekly Income Target: $16,667 / 4 weeks = $4,167 per week

Daily Income Target (assuming a 5-day workweek): $4,167 / 5 days = $833 per day

To reach this goal, explore various avenues. The next step is choosing the right venture that will lead you there. Let's explore further.

**5. Selecting the Right Venture:** Unfortunately, the academic system often fails to teach us how to create wealth. More than merely working hard is required to build substantial wealth. Instead, it's about working smarter, not just harder. Picking the appropriate venture is pivotal in creating a leveraged income business. It entails evaluating various options and selecting the one that aligns best with your goals, skills, and resources.

Let's delve into a detailed exploration of different ventures:

**1) Traditional Employment:**

**Pros:** Offers a stable income stream and benefits like healthcare and retirement plans.

**Cons:** Limited earning potential and minimal leverage. Income is typically tied to the hours worked, with limited opportunities for exponential growth.

**Exception:** Unless you can own shares or equity in the company you work for or participate in a repeat commission plan based on your existing clients or initial efforts. However, these options may only be available to some and are often limited to certain positions or companies.

**2) Start your own business:**

Self-employed/Small Business Owner: Self-employed/Small Business Owner: This category encompasses professionals such as doctors, lawyers, and consultants who manage their practices or small enterprises. Regrettably, my parents found themselves in this group and ultimately retired with financial struggles. They fell into the common trap of trading time for money, and when it came time to exit their businesses, they faced challenges because their expertise and reputation made them difficult to replace.

Medium/Large Business Owner: Owning a business with employees can be rewarding. However, it comes with high risks concerning employee turnover and potential competition. As a business owner, you have leverage. Still, there are challenges, such as the risk of employees leaving for better pay or becoming competitors due to limited income growth.

**Pros:** Starting your own business offers unlimited earning potential and autonomy in decision-making. It provides opportunities to innovate and build a brand.

**Cons:** However, entrepreneurship involves high risk and uncertainty. It requires significant time, effort, and financial investment. Success often depends on market conditions and competitive factors.

### 3) Franchising or Buying an existing business:

Acquiring a business with established systems, a customer base, and cash flow allows scalability. It's a great way to create leveraged income. This option involves less risk than starting from scratch, but it's only available for some due to requiring substantial capital.

**Pros:** Provides access to a proven business model with established brand recognition and support systems.

**Cons:** Requires a significant initial investment and ongoing royalty payments. It also entails limited flexibility in business operations compared to independent entrepreneurship.

### 4) Investing in Existing Businesses and business Partnerships:

Reserved for those with financial stability or many years of specific professional expertise. Partnerships involve joint ventures or investing in start-ups. This option isn't suitable for you if you are starting your working career.

**Pros:** Allows leveraging existing assets, customer bases, and revenue streams. Provides opportunities for passive income and capital appreciation.

**Cons:** Requires careful due diligence and financial analysis. Involves risks associated with business performance and market dynamics.

### 5) Creating Innovative Products or Services:

Celebrity/Inventor: While lucrative, this path is not accessible to everyone and often requires unique talents or expertise. It involves creating a product or service that appeals to the masses, such as becoming a famous singer or actor, developing a social media platform, etc.

**Pros:** Offers the potential for high returns and market disruption. Allows for creative expression and problem-solving.

**Cons:** Involves significant research and development costs. Success depends on market acceptance and competition.

### 6) Marketing and Digital Entrepreneurship:

Starting a marketing company can help you make money by assisting businesses in attracting more customers and increasing sales through marketing partnerships. For example, if you have 100 clients paying $2000 each per month, you could earn a fixed monthly income of $200,000. However, this requires years of experience in the field and knowing how to set up systems and build a team. Typically, people pursue this option after gaining substantial experience.
**Pros:** Provides access to a global audience and cost-effective marketing channels. Allows for flexible growth and adaptation.

**Cons:** Requires knowledge of digital marketing tools and platforms or hiring people who do. Success might take time due to competition.

## 7)Direct Selling/Network Marketing:

This is how I started my entrepreneurial journey in 2000 alongside my job. I began part-time and eventually transitioned to full-time, achieving financial freedom. Direct selling offers an accessible path to success for everyone, regardless of background or experience. Unlike traditional employment, it allows you to work with reputable companies without the usual job hassles. You can run this business from home without needing significant capital upfront. Direct selling provides a level playing field where your efforts determine success, offering multiple income streams and flexibility. Success here isn't concerned about your past – it's all about what you do now. Unlike regular jobs, where getting ahead can be challenging, direct selling is like a game where everyone has a shot at victory, and your success lifts the whole team higher. It's a way for ordinary folks like you to become millionaires, change your story, and join the group of self-made success stories.

To sum up, you don't need to start a new business. Treat yourself as a business. Start wherever you are right now and build a business around what you are doing. I began a direct selling business from home, alongside my job at a courier company, until I created another income stream, then expanded further.

**Pros:**Low Barriers to Entry: Direct selling typically requires minimal upfront investment compared to other business ventures.Rapid Income Growth: With the right strategy and dedication, individuals can experience rapid income growth in direct selling.

Support and Training: Most reputable direct-selling companies offer extensive support and training programs to help new distributors succeed.

Flexible Work Arrangements: Direct selling allows individuals to work on their schedule and from anywhere they choose.

Community and Networking Opportunities: Direct selling fosters community and camaraderie among distributors.

**Cons:**

Stigma and Misconceptions: Direct selling has often been associated with pyramid schemes and unethical business practices, leading to misconceptions and stigma.

Dependency on Company Policies: Distributors are subject to the policies and decisions of the direct selling company they represent.

But compared to challenges faced in other business ventures, collaborating with the right company that is well funded, offers a variety of products and services, and provides training and support is the best option for anybody who wants to step into the world of business and entrepreneurship to grow personally and financially.

**6. Collaborate for Success:**

Learn from those who have already paved the way to success and seek opportunities with existing businesses or ventures that offer leverage. Warren Buffett's strategy of investing in established companies exemplifies the power of collaboration over starting from scratch.

**7. Strategic Networking:** Expand your network daily by leveraging existing referrals and collaborating with business associates to tap into their contacts when entering new markets. Prioritize value by offering it first, avoiding wasting time with nonqualified contacts. Focus on building genuine relationships and adopt a consultative approach rather than pushing sales. Consider joining international networking clubs to broaden your reach and cultivate meaningful connections that offer valuable opportunities, emphasizing mutual benefit. Utilize third-party influence to enhance credibility, especially in unfamiliar markets. Andre's Networking Tip: The quickest way to establish a relationship while networking is to refer business to others promptly, encouraging reciprocity and fostering a spirit of mutual support.

**8. Build a Strong Team and Culture:** Set up clear ways to work, train people well, and create simple, step-by-step guides for growth. Give tasks to others to save time and resources. Use modern tools and outsourcing to make work easier: Direct selling and network marketing have ready-made ways to grow your team and use resources better.

**9. Just Do It:** I didn't wait until I had all the answers. From day one, I took action. I poured my heart into my business daily until it soared. I hustled enough to replace my job's income in just three months. Then, in the following three months, and the next three after, I unlocked a lifetime of freedom.

**10. To move to the next income level, repeat the steps.**

Conclusion: As you build a leveraged income business within 90 days, remember that your success is within reach. Understanding the power of leveraging income and differentiating it from passive earnings lays the groundwork for a resilient financial future. Focusing on creating leveraged income secures stability, freedom, and opportunities for yourself and your loved ones. You're crafting a path to financial independence and personal fulfillment through the outlined steps, shaping your journey with purpose and strategic actions. Collaboration, strategic networking, and team building are allies in pursuing success, amplifying your potential for growth and prosperity.

To conclude this chapter, I'd like to recap the most important questions and points:

**How does leveraging income benefit you?** Leveraging income opens doors to stability, freedom, and endless possibilities, securing your financial future and creating opportunities for yourself and your loved ones.

**Why should you focus on creating leveraged income?** Relying solely on one income source can be risky. Leveraged income offers resilience in a dynamic world, allowing you to earn repeatedly from your efforts and build a legacy of success.

**How can you start building a leveraged income business?** Begin by cultivating the right mindset, setting clear goals, and identifying ventures aligned with your aspirations. Strategic networking, collaboration, and consistent action will propel you towards your goals.

**What are the benefits of direct selling/network marketing?** Direct selling/network marketing offers low barriers to entry, rapid income growth, flexibility, and a supportive community, paving the way for personal and financial transformation.

**How can you progress to the next income level?** Continuously refine your strategies, adapt to changing circumstances, and remain committed to your goals. By leveraging your experiences and embracing new opportunities, you're poised to ascend to new heights of success and fulfillment.

Now, are you ready to reshape your financial future? Take the first step now!

Click the link or visit andreabouzeid.net to grab this invaluable book and embark on your journey to abundance today!

Already have the book? Connect with me and my team today! Click the link or visit https://andreabouzeid.net/appointment to get started. Let's unlock your path to financial freedom together!

# Yuri Cordero

Yuri Cordero, a woman of faith and proud mother of three, serves as Vice President and Executive Producer of Primer Impacto on TelevisaUnivision, the longest-running Spanish-language daily news magazine show in the USA, reaching audiences worldwide. With over 30 years of leadership experience, the Emmy nominated journalist manages national and international teams for news and entertainment projects. A breast cancer survivor, Yuri advocates for early detection, serving on the boards of NBCF, NAMI Miami, and advising for HAAPE. A best-selling author, bilingual international speaker, and leadership mentor, Yuri's impact extends beyond media. She was the Gala Speaker for PVSA Awards, a prestigious White House non-partisan event, and honored as Agent of Impact by the Florida Marlins. Her multifaceted contributions inspire and empower others globally through her in-person appearances, social media, and interviews for outlets in the US and abroad.

SCAN ME

# Chapter 17

# UNLEASH YOUR POTENTIAL: THE KRONOS METHOD

**Yuri Cordero**

Every second counts! Our lives unfold along a timeline, each of us having a predetermined lifespan. While some enjoy longer journeys than others, failing to discern the opportune moments to advance, remain, or take action can obscure our divine purpose. Within this finite existence, there exist rare opportunities, fleeting and unrepeatable. Should one falter, arriving too early or too late to pivotal junctures, the trajectory of their life may irreversibly alter. How often have we missed seizing that perfect opportunity, only to watch it vanish in the blink of an eye, left to memory, never to be captured again?

I live my Kronos Method every single day of my life. In real-world application, "Kronos" is typically used metaphorically to represent the concept of strategically managing time. It has a price and value. In the fast-paced realm of news broadcasting, it holds an immense cost. Every passing second, minute, and hour shapes our daily program. It's an integral part of our routine. With more than three decades dedicated to this vibrant industry, I've gleaned a profound insight: the judicious management of time and resources stands as the anchor of success.

I currently serve as the vice president and executive producer of Primer Impacto on TelevisaUnivision. A ratings leader and longest running Spanish language news magazine show in the United States, 30 years and counting. I have been there 26 of them; even worked with its creator. Upon joining the network, I worked behind the scenes for various shows, including the one I lead, during annual entertainment specials like the Latin Grammys, managing live shots during their scheduled airtime.

Fast-forward to 2016, I was entrusted with the monumental task of managing the logistical coverage of the Papal visit to Mexico. As project manager, I shouldered responsibilities ranging from budget allocation, travel arrangements, selecting live shot locations, organizing transportation, credentials, and security details in a month's time.

With the Pope's itinerary spanning multiple cities across that country, it demanded thorough planning and precise execution.

Faced with tight deadlines and a demanding schedule, my first step was to scrutinize the Pope's itinerary, meticulously noting every destination, date, and time of events. To streamline our operations, I adopted a strategic approach: I orchestrated our travel arrangements to mirror the Pope's own schedule. The Return on Investment (ROI) for this approach was substantial. I assembled a team comprised of experts possessing specialized knowledge and skills, including the lead cameraman, production supervisor, engineers, and security team. We made informed decisions on the spot, minimizing delays by avoiding the need for extensive consultations or deliberations. It simplified our operations, contributed to cost savings, optimized our resources, and reduced downtime.

This comprehensive planning allowed us to condense our coverage into a tight five-day window. The coordination and execution were flawless, resulting in a successful broadcast that captured every moment of the historic visit. This strategic approach to economizing time and resources is a tactic I've employed on several assignments, with positive results, and can be applied in any industry.

In news, there's an inexplicable allure to the day-to-day hustle; the rush of adrenaline coursing through your veins during pivotal moments before a deadline looms, and the broadcast is imminent. In those electrifying instances, every heartbeat seems to echo with purpose: five minutes morphs into an ample window to capture the ideal shot, type the flawless phrase, or air the quintessential story. Each second stretches into an eternity. And when all aligns seamlessly, you exhale. This, my friends, is what I call passion.

Time is passion's silent accomplice, woven into the fabric of our pursuits and desires, infusing each moment with purpose and meaning. It is the steady heartbeat that propels us forward and ignites our soul. The moment has arrived for you to refine your schedule; better yet, step into your destiny. Embark on that project you've postponed, perhaps for months or even years. Time is not within our grasp; it governs our every move. Relentless and unforgiving, it marches on without pause. Once it slips away, there's no turning back!

Think about it: our lives revolve around constraints, largely dictated by our work schedules. It holds a tangible value, quantified by our salaries. As the director of your life, have you ever considered assigning a monetary worth to every passing moment? Adjust your perspective and see yourself as the proprietor of the enterprise that is YOU. Rethink our relationship with time, transforming it from an enemy to an ally! Time possesses the potential to grant us our deepest desires. If we waste it, the repercussions ripple through every aspect of our lives.

In the professional arena, delays in projects, missed deadlines, and inefficient procedures result in wasted resources, profit loss, and missed financial opportunities. Moreover, the competitive landscape waits for no one, and organizations that fail to capitalize on timely opportunities risk falling behind their rivals.

On a personal level, lost time erodes our ability for professional growth, pursue passions, nurture relationships, and cultivate personal development. Moments spent procrastinating or dwelling on past mistakes steal from our potential of a different future. FOCUS on the now. As the clock ticks relentlessly forward, each hour represents a chance to make meaningful memories, achieve personal milestones, or simply savor the joys of life.

The true cost of lost time lies not only in what we fail to accomplish, but also in the intangible toll it takes on our mental and emotional well-being. Chronic stress, anxiety, and feelings of regret often accompany a pattern of wasted time, causing confusion and annihilating our sense of purpose. I witnessed my mother's life shatter into a million pieces when she battled mental illness, steadfast in her refusal to seek medical help for a condition that altered her life. It destroyed her and our family. One of the most commonly cited regrets people express on their deathbeds is related to neglecting personal happiness, avoiding risks, overworking, and not spending time with loved ones.

With The Kronos Method, you will initiate a journey of self-discovery and transformation. It involves recognizing the nature of time by prioritizing tasks and activities accordingly. Adopting a proactive and disciplined approach to time allocation, ensures each moment has a purpose. Mastering it requires a commitment to maximize productivity without sacrificing what you love most. You can unlock the secrets to unleashing your full potential, resulting in both personal and professional success, following these 10 actionable steps:

## Step 1: Embrace Your Power

In the first step of The Kronos Method, we delve into the concept of power—not as dominance or control, but as the ability to influence, inspire, and effect positive change. By embracing our innate power, we can cultivate confidence, assertiveness, and a sense of purpose that propels us toward our goals. This step encourages individuals to recognize their strengths, talents, and unique abilities, and leverage them as a catapult to make a meaningful impact in their lives and others. What's your area of expertise? Use it! There's also undeniable strength in consistency. No one is perfect, but resilience creates excellence, and we all have the ability to excel.

## Step 2: Cultivate Disciplined Obedience

Disciplined obedience is the foundation of effective leadership. In this step, you must align your actions with your values and goals, demonstrating integrity, reliability, and a commitment to excellence. Through disciplined obedience, we gain the trust and respect of others. It emphasizes the importance of integrity, accountability, and ethical leadership, encouraging individuals to lead by example and uphold high standards of conduct in all aspects of their lives. Saving time through disciplined obedience involves adhering strictly to predetermined schedules, tasks, and priorities.

## Step 3: Adopt resilience in Adversity

Developing strategies to bounce back quickly from setbacks and challenges will minimize the time spent dwelling on difficulties. Focus on your goals, move forward with renewed determination, and develop a growth mindset. Embrace failure as a learning opportunity and maintain a positive outlook in the face of adversity. This allows us to persevere and emerge stronger than before. Rather than becoming stuck in a cycle of frustration or indecision, identify potential solutions, evaluate their effectiveness, and take decisive action. Being proactive saves time by avoiding prolonged periods of uncertainty or analysis paralysis. Resilient individuals are better at managing stress, maintain a sense of stability and perspective during difficult times. Maintaining a positive outlook, reduces feeling overwhelmed and avoids burnout.

## Step 4: Harness the Authority of Leadership

Leadership is not just a title, it is a mindset and a set of skills that allow us to inspire, motivate, and guide others toward a common goal. In this step, we explore the qualities of effective leadership, such as empathy, communication, and visionary thinking, and learn how to cultivate them in ourselves and others. It encourages individuals to embrace their role as leaders with integrity, compassion, purpose, and make a positive impact in their families, organizations, and communities. Instead of dwelling on failures or setbacks, leaders acknowledge the situation, learn from it, refocus and move forward.

## Step 5: Embrace Aggressive Patience

Aggressive patience is the art of pursuing our goals with unwavering determination and resilience, while also remaining calm, composed, and adaptable in the face of challenges. In The Kronos Method, we embrace aggressive patience as a strategic approach to achieving long-term success, recognizing that greatness takes time, tenacity, and action. This step emphasizes the importance of walking with patience and resolve to achieve our goals, empowering individuals to stay focused and committed to their vision so when the time comes, they are ready.

I am a God-fearing woman who believes in His time. Habakkuk 2:3 states, "For still the vision awaits its appointed time; it hastens to the end—it will not lie. If it seems slow, wait for it; it will surely come; it will not delay."

Just as a vision has its appointed time, the process of achieving success through The Kronos Method requires you to be prepared. Despite delays or setbacks along the way, individuals are encouraged to trust in the process, remain steadfast in their efforts, and wait for the fruition of their goals. The verse underscores the belief that, in due time, with diligence and commitment, success will be achieved. Keep going!

## Step 6: Master Time Management

Time is a precious resource. In this step, we learn how to prioritize tasks, set realistic deadlines, and eliminate time-wasting activities, maximizing productivity by engaging in what truly matters. The following is a practical technique for managing time effectively to achieve your goals with confidence and competence.

Moving forward, visualize your life as a timeline, shaped by your habits and responsibilities, spanning 16 up to 18 hours a day for some individuals. Break down each hour into 40-minute intervals, allowing 20 minutes for breaks and potential distractions. To implement this method effectively, diligently record your hourly activities for seven consecutive days. While this may seem arduous, it is essential for gaining insight into your time allocation patterns. After the week is complete, analyze the data to identify recurring trends and pinpoint areas where adjustments are warranted.

LEADERS SAY NO. Being selective about commitments and non-essential tasks or requests allows you to prioritize your time for activities that align with your ambitions. Be radical! Challenge yourself, your time commitments, your social circle, cancel unnecessary meetings and reduce your digital consumption habits. If you aspire to acquire new knowledge or skills, you must actively carve out time for learning. Growth often demands sacrifices in time. While routines offer comfort, they can also lead to stagnation.

## Step 7: Route of Execution

Execution is key to turning vision into reality. In this step, we develop a clear plan of action, identifying specific tasks, deadlines, and responsibilities to ensure we achieve our goals. Utilize tools such as calendars, to-do lists, and my time-blocking technique to structure your day effectively. This step emphasizes the importance of taking action and following through on commitments, allowing you to execute plans with precision and achieve desired outcomes. Develop self-discipline by adhering to your schedule, resisting procrastination, and staying committed. Disciplined obedience leads to greater proficiency, allowing you to finish what you start!

## Step 8: Personal Council

Why are you doing it all by yourself? It's time to assemble a personal council: a trusted group of family members, mentors, colleagues, advisors, and supporters who provide guidance, feedback, and encouragement as we navigate the challenges of leadership. Building a support network allows you to cultivate strong relationships and leverage the collective wisdom and experience to achieve your mission. Lean on your pillars for emotional support and practical assistance when needed. By constructing your personal council, you'll uncover the hidden wealth of resources available to you. I vividly recall a session with a woman I was coaching. In just one hour, we unearthed a trove of support and wisdom that had been within her grasp all along. By striving to shoulder every burden alone, we often overlook the wealth of assistance and guidance within arm's reach.

## Step 9: Effective Collaboration

Collaboration is the cornerstone of advancement and triumph. In this step, we cultivate strong relationships, foster open communication, and capitalize the diverse talents and perspectives of our team to achieve shared goals. This step emphasizes the importance of teamwork, encouraging individuals to work together effectively and optimize the strengths of each team member. If you find yourself as the most knowledgeable person at a table of leaders, it's a sign you're not at the right table.

## Step 10: OWN IT!

In the 10th and final step of The Kronos Method, we take ownership of our journey and our outcomes by taking responsibility for our actions and decisions, allowing us to take control of our lives and create the future we desire.

We embrace accountability, take pride in our achievements, and remain committed to continuous growth and improvement without losing ourselves in the process. As someone who has personally grappled with workaholism, I understand the toll it can take on both mental and physical health. For years, I slept with cell phones on my chest, fearing I might miss a crucial call or message. The pressure I was putting on myself, led to a breast cancer diagnosis. It's time to unburden ourselves from this invisible backpack of perpetual busyness and prioritize what needs our immediate attention and what can wait. Own your time, own your decisions, own your actions, own your life. We are intricately designed to achieve remarkable feats. We are fearfully and wonderfully made! It's a battle between you and yourself. Period. No excuses! What would be the price of neglecting this approach?

By following my Kronos Method, you can improve time management, and achieve greater success in your personal, professional, and financial endeavors. Embark on a journey of growth and transformation with me. Follow me on Instagram @yuri_cordero and @iamhighgrace for more information about one-on-one mentoring and group classes, available in both English and Spanish. If you're seeking a voice to inspire and elevate your next event, I invite you to visit www.yuricordero.com

# Sukh Sandhu

Sukh Sandhu is a renowned real estate developer and entrepreneur, known for his visionary approach to projects that positively impact communities. Born into an agricultural, political, and business family, he began understanding the real estate industry at a young age and started a car sales company while studying mechanical engineering. Sukh has completed numerous residential and commercial projects and is known for his ability to find untapped opportunities and turn them into successful businesses. In addition to real estate, Sukh supports education, healthcare, and social welfare charities, aiming to improve neighborhoods beyond his career. His leadership and perseverance have earned him numerous real estate awards, showcasing his excellence, ethics, and creativity. Sandhu values a well-rounded lifestyle that promotes personal growth and enjoyment, including hobbies like travelling, gym-going, golfing & other outdoor activities, and creativity. His dedication, vision, and drive for excellence continue to impact the real estate industry and the communities he serves. His commitment to fostering a culture of creativity has inspired others to think outside the box and push the boundaries of what is possible.

SCAN ME

# Chapter 18

# CHALLENGES AND PITFALLS OF CONSTRUCTION

**Sukh Sandhu**

I immigrated to Canada from India at the age of 19, driven by my aspiration to pursue a career in real estate development. After engaging in a diverse range of manual labor jobs for a year, I have come to understand that life will not be effortless. Upon graduating from Centennial College with an engineering degree, I started a car sales business to fund my continued study. However, I soon realized that achieving my aim was impossible due to a lack of sufficient expertise and access to necessary resources.

Following my graduation, I dedicated five years of my professional career to working for an automobile firm. During this time, I had the opportunity to collaborate with highly intelligent colleagues and receive comprehensive training in demanding management approaches and skills.

After saving for four years, I was able to purchase my first commercial property. Subsequently, I ventured into real estate development, although not before encountering numerous obstacles and pitfalls and nearly going insolvent during the development of one of our largest projects during COVID-19. That moment prompted me to consider how I could assist others in achieving greater success in this industry, given that developers have limited access to information to improve their businesses.

The Construction Industry is a distinctive and challenging business venture where the success of projects relies on various aspects fitting together seamlessly, like a 'complex puzzle'. Each project necessitates substantial funds as well as a team of highly educated, qualified, and experienced consultants and construction specialists. The team members utilize their expertise and understanding not only to advance the project but also to minimize every potential misstep, mistake, or omission that may occur along its course.

In the present intricate and rapidly changing context, every construction company strives to manage, oversee, guide, solve, and build this 'complex puzzle' within the allocated budget and timeframe while meeting all quality standards in construction.

Any unforeseen difficulty or problem that develops during the construction process typically carries the potential for a costly fix. These flaws and issues need to be promptly addressed in accordance with industry standards.

## Most evident and crucial challenges and pitfalls during the pre-construction and building phases:

Unanticipated occurrences, such as accidents, catastrophes, and natural disasters, have the potential to disrupt construction operations and result in delays. Health and safety considerations, along with supplementary precautions to safeguard the building site, might have an effect on project schedules. Malfunctions and technological difficulties: Equipment malfunctions, failures in machinery, and technical concerns have the potential to interrupt construction operations and result in delays. These difficulties may necessitate repairs, replacements, or more time for troubleshooting.

**Change in Design:** At times, the project owner may decide to alter the project's design even before construction begins. This can unintentionally create significant difficulties for the general contractor, affecting all areas of construction, including mechanical, electrical, and structural components of the project. Specifically, it would result in additional expenses beyond the original budget. Inadequate allocation of contingency funds for the project may result in additional delays until the necessary funding gaps can be addressed.

**The Project Surpasses the Budget:** This might arise as a result of unforeseen factors, such as unanticipated alterations in design, fluctuations in material prices, or shortages in labor, which can result in delays and escalated costs. Amidst the COVID-19 pandemic in 2020, the construction industry experienced significant challenges, resulting in severe disruptions to both local and international product supply. Consequently, construction projects faced further delays. Consequently, the trades had delays of several months before receiving their product. Moreover, these delays have resulted in increased costs and placed a significant financial burden on the developers. Furthermore, the contractors were adversely impacted since the scarcity of materials led to an increase in their material expenses. From a contractual standpoint, this can be associated with the concept of "force majeure," but it can have significant and far-reaching consequences for the project. I have witnessed individuals experiencing significant financial losses as a result of these delays, which impose a substantial strain on the project owners. Amidst the ongoing Covid-19 pandemic in 2020, if your project falls under the non-essential category, it would be subject to government shutdowns, resulting in significant cost overruns. The majority of these projects were ineligible for government relief funding due to the mistaken belief that all developers do not require additional help or cash.

**Delays:** Construction projects often encounter delays, which can influence the overall timeline and financial plan. Delays can occur due to various circumstances, including permit delays, adverse weather conditions, labor disputes, or problems in the supply chain. These delays might result in inconvenience for clients and incur additional expenses for contractors. Project delays can arise from several sources; however, they consistently occur and are regarded as one of the utmost critical aspects to monitor in the sector.

To tackle construction delays, it is necessary to employ proactive management, provide excellent communication among all parties involved in the project, and possess the capability to adjust to unforeseen circumstances. To reduce the impact of unforeseen obstacles on construction timelines, it is crucial to engage in meticulous planning, conduct risk assessment, and implement contingency measures.

**Weather:** Weather conditions can have a substantial impact on construction timelines, particularly for projects conducted outside. Inclement weather can jeopardize the personnel's ability to perform their duties, as well as hinder the transportation and delivery of products and equipment. In the initial phase of building, there may be instances of flooding at the site. Dewatering these areas is not only expensive but also challenging due to the properties of water.

**Permit Timeline:** Certain communities are facing a significant influx of new building projects, resulting in delays in obtaining permits and regulatory approvals due to limited staffing or budgetary constraints. Projects can experience delays due to the protracted process of acquiring essential permits and permissions from local authorities. Possible reasons for this delay include a backlog in the permitting process, additional requirements imposed by regulatory authorities, or unforeseen concerns that must be resolved before construction can commence.

**Material Shortages:** Shortages can cause delays in construction projects due to supply chain disruptions and manufacturing concerns. Lack of easily accessible vital resources can impede on-site advancement and prolong project schedules.

**Environmental Issues:** Environmental dangers and soil instability or easements may result in construction delays, as adjustments to the construction plans are necessary to address these issues. Construction schedules may be impacted by environmental restrictions and mandates, particularly in regions that encompass safeguarded habitats or vulnerable ecosystems.

**Poor Management:** Poor management and Insufficient coordination among subcontractors, suppliers, and other project stakeholders can result in scheduling conflicts and subsequent delays. Insufficient communication & planning, and disagreements among various crafts might hinder the advancement of work on the construction site.

**Safety Hazards:** Ensuring the safety of workers is a paramount concern within the construction sector. Construction sites are perilous settings, characterized by multiple hazards such as falls, incidents involving heavy machinery, and exposure to dangerous substances. Implementing adequate safety standards and providing comprehensive training is crucial to minimize these hazards and safeguard the welfare of employees. To effectively implement safety measures, it is essential for the General Contractor (GC) or Project Manager to demonstrate dedication by providing guidance and overseeing safety programs that align with the regulations set by the governing authority or Ministry of Labor.

**Labor Shortages:** Construction projects are dependent on skilled labor, and a scarcity of labor shortages & deficit of proficiency in the workforce can have a substantial influence on project timelines. The scarcity is mostly caused by an aging workforce, diminished interest among younger generations, and competition from other businesses. The paucity of proficient individuals might result in project delays, escalated labor expenses, and difficulties in attaining quality benchmarks. Currently, there is a trend among young people to favor employment possibilities that are considered more socially acceptable. However, this preference is leading to a shortage of trained workers in certain fields. Government entities at various levels must collaborate closely to formulate immigration rules that align with the demands of the real estate development sector. Similarly, the construction industry should collaborate with both labor unions and the government to enhance its reputation and establish vocational schools dedicated to construction skills training. This would effectively promote the benefits and merits of pursuing a highly lucrative career in the building sector.

**Building the Right Team:** Construction projects entail the participation of various stakeholders, such as architects, consultants, contractors, subcontractors, suppliers, and clients. Efficient communication and collaboration among these parties are essential for the seamless advancement of the project. Inadequate communication or a lack of coordination can result in mistakes, the need for additional work, and delays. Effective communication with your team becomes increasingly crucial as projects become more complex. The expertise and understanding possessed by your team are crucial for the successful execution of any development project. Effective communication in design and building procedures must be consistently monitored, enhanced, and applied to ensure a seamless transition from the construction phase to the intended usage of the finished product.

**Technological Challenges:** Even though the construction industry has made significant progress in embracing technological solutions, it still encounters obstacles in fully incorporating advanced tools and procedures. Utilizing advanced technologies such as Building Information Modelling (BIM), project management software, and virtual reality can enhance project efficiency. However, there might be opposition to adopting these technologies or a lack of knowledge among industry professionals due to concerns about integrating them with existing accounting software. This is mainly because some existing programs are prohibitively expensive. Presumably, the latest advancements in AI technologies have the potential to introduce superior and more streamlined programs in the market.

**Lack of Professionalism:** Over the past decade, the construction industry has experienced a boom due to a shortage of available real estate portfolios. This shortage has unintentionally led to a diminished sense of responsibility & ownership among contractors and professionals in the business. They hold the belief that it is acceptable and understandable to be delayed by a few days in responding or getting back to you, due to the high demand in the market. However, this behavior has resulted in significant financial strain on the organizations and unavoidable legal conflicts. This unprofessional conduct must be rectified, as it is crucial to establish professional connections with all contractors. This will ensure that they comprehend your requirements and adhere to the specified timetables. There are numerous exceptional companies that have strong work ethics, provided that you maintain regular communication with them.

**Legal Disputes:** Legal disputes are one of my favorite subjects. I can dedicate an entire chapter to the topic of legal disputes due to its extensive and crucial nature. These challenges often arise outside your control, stemming from the business activities or financial circumstances of the opposing party. Instances of this occurrence can be more frequent than one might anticipate if agreements are not adequately signed and a thorough due diligence is not conducted before contract assignment. The sector, like any other business, has a significant number of unscrupulous individuals. Even insignificant conflicts can require several years to reach a resolution. There is widespread frustration among individuals as a result of significant pressure exerted by various stakeholders in a project to accomplish their objective.

Construction projects must comply with a multitude of local and national construction laws and regulations. Adhering to these requirements can be a laborious and costly process, necessitating meticulous record-keeping and extensive examinations. Noncompliance with regulations may lead to legal issues, penalties, or even the termination of the project. As construction and contracts grow increasingly complex, both parties must conduct their business with a focus on justifying their actions and keeping thorough records.

To ensure the court receives meticulously maintained and finalized records, leading to enhanced efficacy and dependability of expert opinions. A more robust report submitted to the court will expedite the decision-making process. A property may become subject to a lien if the contractor is not remunerated promptly or anticipates a problem with their payments. Even a spurious lien can require several years to be eradicated, leading to significant complications with your financial institution, as they would withhold cash until the lien matter is addressed. If you lack financial stability, your project may be subject to suspension. Financial and contractual disputes encompass disagreements regarding payments, contract terms, and project financing. These disputes have the potential to escalate into legal actions, work interruptions, or alterations in project trajectory, all of which can cause delays.

Successfully managing regulatory standards and compliance necessitates meticulous attention to detail and aggressive involvement with regulatory authorities. To mitigate the danger of expensive delays and legal complications, construction businesses can minimize by keeping up-to-date with regulatory changes, implementing strong safety measures, and fostering a culture of adherence to rules

**Supply Chain Disruptions:** To deal with supply chain disruptions, it is imperative for stakeholders in the construction sector to have comprehensive backup plans, expand their sources of materials, and cultivate strong connections with suppliers to minimize the consequences of possible disruptions. Adopting cutting-edge technologies like Building Information Modelling (BIM), prefabrication, and drone technology can improve efficiency, precision, and safety in construction projects. Moreover, allocating resources towards the education and enhancement of proficient workers, alongside advocating for inclusivity and diversity in the labor force, can effectively mitigate labor scarcities and stimulate industrial expansion.

To summarize, the construction sector encounters numerous obstacles and dangers that might impede efficiency, safety, and the achievement of project goals. Supply chain interruptions, skilled labor shortages, technical restrictions, and regulatory difficulties necessitate thoughtful analysis and proactive approaches to surmount. Moreover, delays might be caused by productivity problems resulting from inefficiencies, lack of collaboration, or inadequate management.

Although the construction sector faces substantial challenges and risks, it also offers prospects for innovation, enhancement, and sustainable expansion. To overcome these challenges and succeed in a constantly changing global environment, the industry should implement proactive strategies, embrace technology improvements, and prioritize safety and quality.

**How can we help:**

Our construction management and property management teams have a longstanding history of 20 years. I can assist individuals in constructing real estate properties in Ontario by prioritizing many essential aspects. My team provides various insights into the commercial and residential construction, rezoning, site selection & acquisition, municipal planning, design planning, repositioning the property, project budgeting and financial structuring.

We shall discuss the regulations and taxes pertaining to real estate development in Ontario. Examples of these include zoning regulations, building laws, development charges, and project authorizations. It is imperative for anyone engaged in real estate development within the province to possess a comprehensive understanding of these regulations and adhere to them accordingly.

In addition, my team can provide support in identifying sustainable development prospects in Ontario and integrating environmentally friendly design, planning & energy efficiency, into real estate projects. Our approach to real estate development ensures active participation and collaboration with local communities, stakeholders, and government agencies in every project.

We can provide further guidance in obtaining approval for development projects, commencing from conceptualization and design, up to the acquisition of municipal permits and clearances. To be successful, you must possess a comprehensive understanding to prevent any potential delays and adhere to all necessary regulations. Individuals in need of financial support for their projects may find it advantageous to investigate opportunities for collaboration, alliances, and investment in ownership shares.

By implementing the tips and techniques outlined in this chapter, you will not only enhance the quality of your work but also streamline your processes and improve efficiency. Remember, every project is an opportunity to learn and grow. So, embrace challenges, stay curious, and let your passion for construction drive you towards excellence. Here's to building a brighter, more innovative future, one carefully laid brick at a time.

# Alan P. Hill

**Alan P. Hill** is a Property Investor, International Speaker & Trainer and a Best-Selling Author.

He faced **setbacks that would crush most people,** then forged a multi-million property empire and an **unshakeable legacy.**

After bouncing back from rock bottom, Alan is living proof that **smart strategy and sheer determination matter more than luck.** He turned a devastating blow into a mission to protect & empower entrepreneurs and **that's what's making Alan and his clients wealthy - right now.**

For the past 15 years, Alan has been helping Entrepreneurs and High Performers generate **truly passive income,** secure their future and **build their legacy.**

But Alan believes building wealth serves a **bigger purpose.** He has collaborated with titans of personal development, including: **Tony Robbins, Robert Kiyosaki, Blair Singer, T Harv Eker and Brian Tracy.**

His story is proof **you can rewrite your future.**

SCAN ME

# Chapter 19

# INTENTIONAL WEALTH

## HOW TO SECURE YOUR FUTURE, BUILD YOUR LEGACY, AND SUPERCHARGE YOUR INCOME

### Alan P. Hill

*"Every adversity, every failure, every heartache carries with it the seed of an equal or greater benefit."*
Napoleon Hill

New Year's Day 2020 shattered my world. **"I'm so sorry, but we think you have Brain cancer,"** the nurse said.

Fear gripped me, I thought of my wife and my 9-month-old son. Would I need to record some videos so that he could at least know something of me?

Days of tests confirmed not cancer, but a brain bleed…I had experienced a kind of stroke called a "Cavernous Hae-mangioma" on my cerebellum.

Relief was very short-lived, uncertainty still staring me in the face. I could not walk or even read. Would I ever recover? Hospitalised for a month, weakness and pain became my constant companions. My life shrunk to basic tasks, a stark contrast to the freedom I cherished.

Throughout this whole nightmare, there was one thing I never thought about or worried about…**I never worried about money.**

## A fate worse than death?

I made a full recovery within about 3 months. But what I learned from my experience in hospital was a harsh truth:

**I realised that for entrepreneurs who value freedom, autonomy, and personal control—there is <u>a fate worse than death.</u> That is to be lying sick in a hospital bed, watching helplessly at the sidelines, as your family begins to circle the drain financially…and there's nothing you can do about it.**

Regardless—so many high performers and entrepreneurs are fantastic at making money. But if you are sick for any period and have a family to support, especially if you have already achieved a certain lifestyle—what then?

## Mission "Protection, Freedom and Wealth"

Fuelled by this realisation, I embarked on a new mission: empowering current and aspiring entrepreneurs and high performers to build true passive income through specifically designed, strategically selected, and personally curated property investments.

This is a safety net—one that grants freedom, knowing your family is protected even if you can't work.

But it's not just about protection. It's also about **freedom and wealth.** The freedom to live the lifestyle of your choosing—and not just through income, but by creating wealth and **building a legacy the way the elite have done for generations.**

Imagine pursuing your passions, travelling the world, or simply spending quality time with loved ones, all because your finances support your choices. That's why I created my business mission:

**I help entrepreneurs and high performers to build security and passive income, and to create a legacy through real, passive, wealth-creation, so that they can enjoy freedom of choice and live the lifestyle they deserve and desire.**

Does that sound like something of interest to you?

If so, whether you are an entrepreneur or a high performer, or whether you aspire to be one; you are in the right place, with the right book, at the right time. One of my mentors once told me:

> *"When the student is ready the teacher will appear."*
>
> Lao Tzu.

So, are you ready? If so, consider this chapter your guide, offering strategies and insights to get you moving towards (or faster towards) true financial freedom.

## Stumbling blocks or stepping stones?

Now I did not get into investing personally to show off, I could have bought several supercars by now, and honestly, I was tempted. Instead, I chose to take a humble investment that is beautiful and valuable, one which provides a **wonderful home for someone else** and **creates freedom and opportunity for me.**

And you can start small. Did you know it is possible to start with £100 cash and invest in a crowdfunded property project, or that certain properties in the UK can be bought with less than £15,000 deposit.

So, what led me to create several multi-million-pound businesses **and** a passive income producing, multi-million-pound property portfolio over the past 20 years?

Experiencing a stroke was the third significant event in my life that led me to look for ways of turning challenges into opportunities. The first major event was when our family of six became homeless after losing the family home in the 1991 recession.

When I started my working life, I dedicated myself to study and learn all I could about property to make sure it never happened to me—how **not to lose.**

**But the other side of that coin is, of course, how to win.** I studied house prices back to World War 2, and interest rates back to the inception of the Bank of England in 1694—and I found the ways to not only **minimise risk,** but also to **make significant profits.**

So now I have the freedom to spend my time when, where and how I want,—doing what I want and living my mission. That includes helping a select group of business owners and high performers to do the same.

## Ask the future you.

The key insight I want you to take away from this chapter is this: **anyone can create passive income and massively grow their wealth,** just like I have done and like all those I have helped do the same.

But if you miss one of the key elements, you will fail, struggle, or just stagnate. I have seen it all too often in the last decade or so. Not only that—**most people won't take action.** Not everyone is ready. That part alone takes 95% of people out of the game…

So, what about you? Where do you want to be in five, ten or twenty years' time? Is the 'future you' thanking you, glad you moved forward? Or regretting you didn't?

### Is "millionaire" your benchmark, not your ceiling?

Clarity is power; so, what is **your definition** of financial freedom?

One of my mentors says this:

> *"Once my monthly cashflow from my assets is equal to or greater than my monthly living expenses, then I am financially free because my assets are cash-flowing and are working for me."*
> Robert Kiyosaki

So many people these days talk about well-known mentors like they are best friends, they'll show a photo of them smiling together at a seminar. All I will say is, just have a peek at my website alanphill.com to **see examples of my direct collaborations** with legends **Tony Robbins, T. Harv Eker**, **Robert Kiyosaki**, **Blair Singer** and of course **Brian Tracy.**

Working with any one of these major leaders in this business of personal development could be considered a fluke, twice—good luck, but five times? That is a pattern.

I say this not to impress you, I say it because all this comes from someone who started out 20 years ago homeless—

with nothing but a black plastic bin bag full of clothes, donated to me by the local church. If you are in a stronger starting position than that—**where might you be able to end up?**

My point is that it's **no mistake** that I have excelled in these three areas of business, property and international speaking and training—all connected by the overarching bridge of **ongoing financial education**, one of the key ingredients for financial success in any field.

**If you only take away one thing from this book, make it <u>a new commitment</u> to become a <u>permanent student of your financial education.</u>**

Would you be willing to do that? If so—I will shortly be giving you a gift for you to help you make and keep that commitment to yourself.

## <u>The Problem</u>

So, what holds most successful people back (including me in the beginning)? Working with thousands of entrepreneurs and high performers over the years, I have identified that, despite their success, they face three key problems:

**1. Income Insecurity:** They depend on their own activity for income, creating financial risk—which itself causes an additional pressure that only increases the risk of health issues.

**2. Lack of Diversification:** They often rely on a single sector, so they are vulnerable to the rapid changes we are now seeing more of in the world.

**3. Missed Opportunities:** They neglect **two of the greatest most life changing wealth-building tools;** one was dubbed "the 8th wonder of the modern world" by Albert Einstein, but I will explain them both here shortly,

## <u>The Solution</u>

The wealthy mitigate these problems by generating multiple sources of passive income, primarily through **very specific types of property investments.** It requires understanding of a select few key investment strategies that maximise returns, coupled with **knowing how to uncover under-valued deals.**

**This is exactly what I show people how to do** so you end up with less risk, stronger financial security, and a platform to **build your net worth rapidly and exponentially,** and so you can leave a truly lasting legacy.

So, let's look at that three-fold challenge I identified and set out your action steps to overcome them, knowing that if you do, you are **well on your way to financial freedom.**

## Income Insecurity & Lack of Diversification

If you want an unbeatable way of smashing through the first 2 of these top challenges—the simple formula is to use profits, bonuses, or savings—and invest into a specific type of income-producing property investment—one that produces a **significantly higher profit** than most and leads to the **fastest way to financial freedom.**

In short, to kill the first two challenges with one stone, **keep focused on what you are great at making money doing**—and j**ust use property to diversify into new passive income streams** so you have income even if you can't work. This simple formula has provided me with a very stable income over the last few decades—regardless of the challenges out there in the world.

In fact—**my property income was unaffected by the COVID outbreak in 2020**—all because of how it was set up. Not many people can say that.

By diversifying into property, you create an extra layer of protection, but even if you are already in property—people will always need a place to live.

## Missed Opportunities

The third of these challenges is absolutely the strongest and **most exciting** one to overcome, and it can be **fully passive and automatic.**

For those that already know me through my online membership site, or who work with me 1:1 to help them find the highest performing properties in the market—you already know what I am talking about. Let's look at power of two of the most **life changing** concepts you can learn: **compounding** and **leverage**.

Benjamin Franklin, described compounding like this:

> *"Money makes money. And the money that money makes, makes money."*
> Benjamin Franklin

That is the simplest explanation of compound interest you'll ever hear. And as for leverage, entrepreneur J.C. Penney described it as "one of the greatest business multipliers I know."

My personal take is this:

> *"Financial leverage is when you borrow money to make more money. Leverage is like using a magnifying glass in strong sunlight—it can magnify your gains, but it can also burn you if you're not careful!"*
> Alan P. Hill

## Why go for 10x when 27x is standard?

Here is an example of leverage and compounding working beautifully together. Let's use a simplified example from the UK, where you bought an £80,000 house with a 25% deposit in January of 2000.

That is £20,000 of your own money and the other £60,000 (75% of the house price) is leverage—it is debt. Of course, the rental income must more than cover mortgage payments, but in the UK the lenders will check this for you, so you don't risk a negative cashflow.

The average property value in the UK has gone from £77,000 in the beginning of 2000, up to £259,000 in 2023.

**That is 333% growth in 24 years**—more than triple the value. But **you actually get twenty-seven times growth.** How does that work...?

You simply take "additional borrowing" three times between 2000 and 2024, with enough tax-free cash coming out to reinvest and **double your property portfolio each time you refinance.** One house becomes two, then two becomes four and then four becomes eight. **This is exponential growth, the magic of compounding** in action—together with leverage.

When property values get to £270,000 – the third time you refinance you will have eight houses worth well over £2.1 million (up from £80,000) and your equity is no longer £20,000 like it was in 2000,—but a whopping £540,000.

**Forget "10x"—this is 27x,** meaning you now have **twenty-seven times the value of your initial investment (2700%).**

And this is **on top of any monthly cashflow** from rental income. Now do you see why the wealthy like property?

### A gift to you, from Brian Tracy and I

That was a simplified example—really all I can do in one chapter, but for those who are already learning with me, you know that the maths and reality do agree with one another.

I have been investing for 20 years so I experienced the 2008 crash (and the subsequent recovery), and my own portfolio survived and still followed the compounding growth patterns illustrated above. So, as I like to say about compounding, "if it's good enough for Einstein, it's good enough for me!"

If you also want to maximise profit and minimise risk, you will need to make a series of decisions which I break down for you in my online programme which **you can get access to today, as my gift to you,**—my gratitude for buying (and actually reading) this book, and my congratulations to you for committing to invest your time, energy, and money in yourself.

Just go to www.alanphill.com/briantracygift and I will help you create and maintain your new financial education habit, so you get all the value you need (spaced out in bite-sized chunks, so you don't get overwhelmed) including:

1. How to buy property in the UK when you **live abroad** (like me)

2. How to borrow **millions of "good debt"**—without a huge salary.

3. How to make it **truly "passive"** with **positive cashflow** (many fail on this part).

4. How to use **advanced strategies** like the wealthy.

5. How to consistently win **huge discounts** on purchases – with integrity.

6. And so much more...

Earlier I mentioned being homeless and having to go through black plastic bin bags full of donated clothes. That's because there was one other massive life challenge I had to face up to as I was coming of age as a young man. Now is not the right time to go into that, but if you'll allow me, I'd love to share more with you—not only my own story, but also inspirational successes my students have all achieved too.

If you would be willing to accept my gift to you go to www.alanphill.com/briantracygift so we can stay connected, and you can keep learning.

So, are you ready to take a step forward, to create the life-style you desire and deserve?

***"The act of taking the first step is what separates the winners from the losers."***

Brian Tracy

So, what will your first step be?

# Paulo Pereira

Paulo Pereira is a luminary in the convergence of Data Science, Digital Marketing, and Innovation. With certifications from Berkeley, Columbia, and Harvard, Paulo stands at the forefront of the digital transformation era. As the founder of desbrava.ai and a seasoned investor in various start-ups, he brings a wealth of experience and a visionary approach to enhancing business performance through cutting-edge data and digital strategies. His career is highlighted by the development of a unique methodology that has been applied across diverse niches and companies, achieving significant impact in collaboration with giants like Netflix, Walmart, and Warner Bros. Beyond his professional achievements, Paulo's role as a Content Creator and Certified AI Consultant underscores his passion for leveraging technology to optimize business outcomes. His extensive research and immersive programs across global markets from Silicon Valley to Singapore reflect his commitment to empowering businesses through social analytics, trend analysis, and the strategic application of AI and digital marketing insights.

# Chapter 20

# THE POWER OF DATA-DRIVEN MARKETING AND SALES IN THE DIGITAL AGE

**Paulo Pereira**

## The future of the past of the present

The one thing that made me transform careers and leave behind one of the most comfortable chairs in the entertainment market was to wholeheartedly believe in the marriage between data and digital marketing. In my head, that was the future.

It was 2017 when I started to get impatient with the way I, as Director of Marketing and Commercial at the 2nd largest cinema chain in Brazil and the world, invested my budget in the digital market. We had no metrics, comparisons, or in-depth data analysis. It was rivers of money for influencers, without even knowing the return.

The chair was indeed comfortable; besides being a Herman Miller, it placed me as one of the main executives in the cinema industry in the country. Once I put my ego aside, I started to invest time and money in knowledge about the two topics to get to the perfect match: data and digital.

As I was in line to assume the presidency of the company, my bosses invested in a Leadership and Management training at Harvard Business School, where I was able to get a broader view of the international business world. Subsequently, on my own, I went to invest in the two topics, first in a specialization in Digital Marketing and Analytics, from Columbia University.

## A soldier when he returns from war

But it was in 2018, when I found what I know as the best Data Science education in the world, the specialization from Berkeley University. There I had the opportunity to immerse myself in companies like Netflix, Singtel from Singapore, Walmart, the Oakland Athletics baseball team that originated the movie Moneyball with Brad Pitt. Imagine just that, me meeting Billy Beane in his office in San Francisco, long after it premiered in theaters…

When I returned to Brazil, I made the analogy with a soldier returning from the war to his job. There was no way of going back to being the same, following the same old routines; I started to want to change everything in the company and the market but, obviously, in traditional markets closed to change and innovation, in addition to not investing in futurism, everything ended up going down the drain.

As a result, I resigned in March 2019. This is where the journey of desbrava.ai began, a technology startup focused on digital, with the aim of empowering people and companies to make better decisions and strategies based on data and not make the same mistakes I did. With all the knowledge, I had gained from working in large companies and studying with great scientists from more than 15 countries, my goal was to shorten the path of executives and entrepreneurs in this universe.

## Looking where everyone looks and seeing what no one sees

A leader is only a leader once he knows where he wants to go—I always had this phrase with me, and it was when I looked at what companies in Asia, Europe, and America were doing, knowing that Brazil was still far behind in innovation, that I realized that I and all my competitors were trying to present data, descriptive and diagnostic analyses, that is, what happened and how it happened.

I realized that to bridge the technology gap with large enterprises, I needed to focus on delivering actionable insights to customers, preferably with a strategic direction already in place. That means focusing on the most complex, but most valuable, analytics, which are predictive and prescriptive—what will happen and what to do when it happens.

Before ChatGPT burst onto the scene in early 2023, we'd been struggling for two years to incorporate artificial intelligence into our customers' universe. It was, however, difficult, and the success of OpenAI helped us a lot in raising people's awareness. Because it has .ai in its name, our website traffic literally exploded. We started to focus on the problem that people didn't even know they had, instead of focusing on the solution. That's when business started to pick up.

If you understand the marriage between data and digital, you come to the conclusion that, just like in a marriage, each has its strengths and weaknesses. They are there to complement each other, and when they reach the ideal harmony, they achieve a more prosperous life, reap fruit, have children, and provide all the security and direction for them to grow in the right way. It's a beautiful analogy and very real.

Once I understood this, I began to lay down some foundations for my ideas, and I came up with a few key principles for succeeding in this environment.

**The 5 Principles of Success for Capturing and Retaining Customers in the Digital World:**

**1. Access Strategies:**

Take off your executive hat and put on the consumer one. What comes to your mind?

The first questions you ask might be: I want to know, I want to go, I want to do, I want to buy, right?

Now put your executive hat back on and think, how to be there when your customer asks these questions. How to be faster than the competition when this happens, how to be more relevant in that micro-moment, what are the right channels that will provide access for your customer to reach you.

We need to think about these micro-moments with the goal of being accessible to customers when they are looking for something you provide.

This is why it is important to apply multichannel strategies. Here comes another methodology I developed over these years of research and studies: the 5Cs of Knowledge Methodology.

You need to know everything about the profiles and interests of your Customers, about the Channels to reach them, the right Content for each of these channels and customers, the strengths and weaknesses of the Competition, and all the Costs involved in this ecosystem.

Put all the points raised in these 5Cs into a mind map or matrix to help you visualize, and you will have the knowledge you need to define your access strategies. Many people message me later to say that this is a foolproof exercise. Don't fail to do the same, contact me to discuss this practice if you need further information.

## 2. Engagement Strategies:

If you were born before the 90s, you will remember the Broadcast Era, when we had excessive attention but scarce content.

Today, in the Abundance Era, we have attention scarcity but excessive content. Quite a game-changer, isn't it?

And how to generate engagement in this content war across multiple platforms, and still compete for people's time and attention?

This is where I reinforce that the 5Cs of Knowledge methodology goes hand in hand with these 5 strategies to capture and retain customers. Once you have identified all the points in the exercise above, you will certainly know how to engage your customer more easily in the digital environment.

Many clients sometimes tell me: "Paulo, I have an excellent digital presence, take a look at my Instagram profile to understand."

And when I go through everything, I see that they lack a better and faster website, presence on other social networks, do not have a well-defined traffic strategy, do not have direct channels of customer relationship like chatbots, newsletters, etc.

So, how can you discuss digital presence by acting on a single social network?

Think of the digital world as a shopping mall: if your store doesn't attract the customer in that corridor, they will enter another one. Furthermore, if your store closes its doors, you may not have another source of customer relationship, and the mall certainly won't feel a thing if your store closes, especially because it has several others in the same niche.

### 3. Customization Strategies:

When you have a complete understanding of your customers through thorough data analysis, and know what content to use on each channel to reach them, you can achieve one-to-one segmentation—speaking directly to each customer in a personalized, rather than generalized, way.

Defining your key personas is important. But thereafter, you can actually tailor your communications differently to each customer.

This is where streaming and e-commerce companies have differentiated themselves, in one-to-one segmentation.

Now, there are strategies that don't require as much data. Remember the case of Coca-Cola, where you could find cans with your name on them?

Or the irreverent Starbucks style of writing the customer's name on the cup?

The digital environment is the conducive environment that big companies have built to give you the opportunity to get closer to your customers. Take advantage of it, and it's free; you only pay when you need and want to do something more amplified.

## 4. Connection Strategies:

You are ready. You've done your homework, analyzed and defined assertive strategies to engage your customer. The result is automatic, you can trust it.

Customers will connect with you because you have created value for them and made them consider you as an option.

They often reach this point of consideration already with a sense of belonging, with all objections removed, and with a very high level of awareness of what you offer.

And if that connection is genuine, one of the things that happens most with companies that reach that level is a sense of community. Going back to streaming and e-commerce, aren't they the ones that are really engaging with their customers on social media? So now you'll understand that to get to that level, the previous steps are highly critical.

I love the conversations of Netflix, Disney, Amazon, and others who are interacting with customers and often even chatting with each other to amplify the message, even though they're competitors. And who hasn't seen screenshots of conversations between them on social media, right?

## 5. Collaboration Strategies:

There's no way around it, a satisfied customer who is part of a community and has a strong sense of belonging will become your collaborator. Better still, they'll be your number one salesperson.

Let's talk about Waze, Spotify, and Netflix again.

You probably thought you were standing out by sharing your Spotify and Netflix passwords with your friends, didn't you? "Hey, look how cool this is. Access, you can use my password, you can't miss out".

Then they kept collecting more and more data, storing all the interests of more and more people, where they were accessing it from, and bringing in more and more customers. Until one day…

And then Waze created so much value for us that we actually felt guilty if we didn't collaborate by reporting radars and accidents.

And I can't see these collaboration strategies without going through the other four strategies first, and also without visualizing the 5Cs of knowledge alongside all of this.

Doesn't that make sense? Wherever I do this in parallel and list these strategies, people say, "Wow, now it all makes sense, let's go and apply this".

And weeks or months later they come to me to tell me their results. 100% of the time they are positive!

**And Action!!!**

Imagine yourself in the daily routine of your decisions, goals, anxiety for growth, fleeing from scarcity at some point; imagine yourself falling behind in the market, and, in addition to this whirlwind of responsibilities and emotions, you come across thousands of gurus selling ease on the internet.

You start running in circles, seeing no real progress in what you know is the way, data and the digital environment as a channel to attract and retain customers.

Let me give you a practical example. Personally, when I was at Singtel, I understood how the lawful monitoring of people's behavioral data could tremendously improve a company's results and even open doors to other markets. Singtel is the largest telecommunications and internet provider in Singapore and Southeast Asia, with over 700 million customers, or about 10% of the world's population at the time, and they entered the content and streaming market because they had billions of user data.

When I was at Netflix in Los Gatos, California, I was amazed at their ability to extract value from data. In one of the conversations with executives, they mentioned that at the time (this was 2018) they were processing over 140,000 data variables to understand the behavior, interests, and potential of each customer. The day and time of consumption are examples of variables, as well as the weather and temperature that day in that neighborhood. Imagine crossing over 140,000 data points like these to decide what to offer the customer when they sit on the couch and turn on the TV… It's very powerful.

Now, if you think of your business as a sponge that absorbs all the data from all the different points of contact with your customers, in each channel, what content works best, how each competitor does it, what costs are involved in each journey, and as you analyze and make decisions, you will understand that data can be one of the richest assets of your business, alongside customers and employees.

All of these companies are not content and retail companies, they are data companies, and their market value is directly linked to the amount of information they hold.

Any company, regardless of size, can use the same strategies we have discussed here; what will change is the proportion and quantity of data. But the value generated for the customer will be the same.

I can just see your mind racing with these strategies. You must be thinking about your "mall store", walking towards the exit and coming to the mall door. It's the approach door that opens automatically when you get close to it. The moment it opens, you see what's on the other side, but if you don't take the next step, it closes again.

I'm sure of one thing. The moment you take that step, the door will automatically close behind you, and you'll be in a different, much wider environment. You won't be able to see yourself differently, like a soldier returning from war: much more experienced, more resilient, with a wide and quick vision, and above all, seeing problems that were once giants as much smaller.

Go ahead, soar in the digital world, revisit these exercises above, remember the cases, and of course, if you have any questions along the way, I'll be more than honored to answer and support you personally. Just drop me a line on any of my channels.

# Toni Isabel Rebic

Toni Isabel Rebic, M.A., Alignment Psychologist since 2005, is the founder of TrueSelf Psychology—a progressive awakening approach that teaches how to align the conscious and subconscious minds to reach centeredness and optimize your level of productivity in the pursuit of your ambitions, the benefits of which have been expressed by numerous clients and online class participants who've reported greater emotional self-mastery, clarity of mind and focus, problem-resolution skills, mindful decision-making, go-getting energy, and more satisfying accomplishments. TrueSelf Psychology has grown into an authentic way of good-living, self-empowerment and goal achievement. As a leader in her field, Toni is regularly invited as a guest speaker and trainer on her alignment teachings, spreading her philosophy that: The better you feel, the better you perform… and the better life gets! Toni can be reached via trueself-psychology.com.

# Chapter 21

# THE POWER OF EMOTIONS IN BUILDING YOUR BUSINESS AND REACHING YOUR GOALS

**Toni Isabel Rebic**

Everyone has goals they want to achieve.

Some will reach their targets, but unfortunately, many will not.

This is not because they're not smart enough, incompetent, or don't have the right skills. It is neither from lack of resources nor opportunities—although those can obviously make reaching target objectives somewhat easier.

Ask someone why they are not achieving their goals, and they'll say it's because they're just unmotivated to do the task, confused by where to start and what to do, overwhelmed with all the responsibilities involved with the project, frustrated by the limited resources at their disposal, intimidated by a demanding boss, or being at odds with employees who don't chip in…

When listening to such complaints, most people would ascribe these as difficult work conditions, highlighting that the task was understimulating, that there were too many responsibilities to deal with, that working with limited resources is taxing, or that it's hard to put up with a pushy boss, or teammates who lack the team spirit.

In other words, people tend to blame their problems on something that's happening to them, from the outside… like on tasks, responsibilities, limited resources and so on.

But in doing so, they concurrently ignore an important aspect of goal achievement that is often overlooked and essential to success:

They don't feel good in the pursuit of what they want.

This may be a little startling, as we tend to believe that we'd feel good having what we want.

But getting there—the journey itself, is another emotional ride.

You can think of a goal but feel insecure about how to make it happen, or uncertain you ever will. You may be concerned that you'll fail, afraid of what people may say if you did, and apprehensive about performing in front of your peers. Some will feel anxious facing the unknown, or overwhelmed by the many challenges they must overcome in order to reach their objectives.

What you want is usually not the problem.

In fact, accomplishing your desires will likely improve your quality of life, work or relationships—by having that dream home, a bonus for work well done, a supportive and loving partner, a growing family, more travel time, or savings set aside for your kids' college funds or your retirement.

However, when thinking of our goals, we typically don't tend to ask ourselves how we would feel in the pursuit of them.

Yet, it is your emotions that determine whether you move towards your objectives, or whether they prevent you from going after them.

I once asked someone who was zealously describing the white Cadillac she'd buy if she ever won a million dollars, if she believed she could win?

She paused for a moment, then looked up at me and replied, "No, I don't."

And that's what most people feel at some point when striving towards what they want—a resistance to their desires.

This came from the mindset of a woman who had worked hard all her life as she often struggled financially. Making easy money was not a construct in her mind. So, her disbelief was stronger than her desire to win.

This energy split between what you want and your limiting beliefs is the source of many broken dreams.

You may even begin to criticize your goals, lamenting that, "It's too hard", "It's not

realistic", or "Who am I to want this!"... which ultimately stops you from feeling good about pursuing them.

But your goals don't create your feelings. Your opinions of them do. Your perception of yourself in achieving them, do. Your beliefs, expectations, and standards all contribute to what you tell yourself when you think of your goals, and therefore how you feel about them.

Thinking good feelings-thoughts about what you want and believing it, feels good; thinking good-feeling thoughts about what you want while not believing it, doesn't.

Most people say that if they win a million dollars, they would pay off their debts, give some to family and a favorite charity, then go off on a long vacation.

So, the goals themselves are not typically the problem. But how to stay emotionally in line with them, often is.

According to a recent study by *Dr. Michelle Rozen, only 6% of people ever fully reach their goals.

That's a staggeringly low number when you think of how happy the world would be if more people lived out their dreams.

But to reach your goals, you must first resolve the negative emotions that hold you back from achieving them. And unfortunately, many don't know how to do that, or even realize they need to.

Many tend to look outward to justify their problems. "It's because I don't have enough time"... "My colleagues are difficult to work with"... "My boss doesn't appreciate me"... which is a main reason why so many get stuck where they are.

You can't change your situation by pointing the finger outside yourself. You lose your power in doing so.

As a solution, some people turn to positive thinking, hoping it'll wash the negative ones away. On repeat: I am good! I am strong! I am successful!

How's that working for ya?

One of the hardest things to do is to feel good about what you want when you can't even see yourself achieving it.

Not all positive thoughts feel good.

Even a compliment can hurt if you don't believe it.

Positive thoughts can only be accepted when you're emotionally close enough to convince yourself they could be true. Otherwise, if you're too far off, resistant thoughts will activate within, triggering feelings of disbelief and discomfort, making you push the positive thoughts away.

You can't just think positive thoughts. You have to feel good about the thoughts you think about.

You want to think better-feeling thoughts that align with your authentic self and what you want, rather than pump-me-up positive ones.

If saying positive mantras was all you needed to be motivated and energized to reach your objectives, there wouldn't be a need for psychologists, therapists, or life coaches.

But emotional help is needed more than ever, as we now have hundreds of studies that support the connection between our emotions with our levels of productivity and goal commitment.

You can tell how close you are to your goals—or whether you'll even achieve them, by how you feel when you think or talk about them.

Haven't you ever heard someone talk about their goals, and you could just feel how close they are to realizing them? And with someone else, it just felt more like wishful thinking?

You can feel a forward-moving momentum when someone speaks excitedly about their goals, versus when someone is describing a goal they don't yet feel. The energy here feels more stagnant.

Maybe you've even heard yourself mention your goals and personally experienced that sinking feeling? Some ascribe this to the imposter syndrome, which often leads to fears that others will see right through them.

But when your emotions are in sync with what you want, you feel unstoppable.

You get this impulse to pick up the phone and make the call, sit down and write that proposal, take a chance and pitch your ideas, reach out to those who could help you, and trust yourself to make things happen.

The pathway to your goals is so invigorating and purpose-driven, that you daydream about them longer, and enjoy the details unfolding in your imagination before actualizing them into physical form.

But if instead, you feel a dissociation between what you want and your journey there, you'll feel nervous when giving a group presentation, apprehensive about cold calling a potential client, and self-conscious about how you appear to your colleagues.

So basically, the more your thoughts are unaligned with what you want, the more resistance you feel in the form of negative emotions against yourself, against taking any action, which consequently will affect your performance and your self-confidence.

That's why it's so important to take care of how you feel.

Ask yourself: Do you perform better when you feel confident or nervous? Happy or sad? Encouraged or pressured?

Undoubtedly, you know you perform better, the better you feel.

There is a quote that says, "Attention goes where energy flows".

But what exactly is that energy? Where does it come from?

Energy comes from your thoughts, and you know what you're thinking by how you feel.

Some will say, you just need to Suck it up! Just get the job done!

Denial has been the source of many broken dreams. Avoidance even more.

Ignoring how you feel is like carrying an unnecessary weight on your shoulders while climbing a mountain. It feels hard, heavy, and slows you down. Maybe even stopping you if you get too tired.

Feeling anxious will hold you back from speaking out; feeling small will keep you behind everyone else; feeling incompetent will increase the number of errors you make. Feeling helpless can make you give up on your goals.

Then by the end of the day, like so many other days when you felt inadequate, you'll review your performance with self-criticism, and ruminate over the mistakes you've made.

The more you think more about what you did wrong, didn't do right, and what you should have done instead, you'll sink deeper into discouragement and helplessness, emotions not in sync with pursuing your goals, but resistant to taking further steps.

You just won't feel like it.

How you feel when you pursue what you want is the most important variable in deciding whether or not you're going to take repeated action in its direction.

You can have a degree on your wall, resources in your bank account, and all the support in the world, but if you don't believe you can have what you want, or feel deserving of it, good enough to have it, you won't take any consistent actions towards its fulfillment.

And without moving in the direction of what you want, you will also not attract the right people, circumstances and events that will help you along the way.

Life rewards action. And action is preceded by emotion.

Most people are just unaware it happens this way. Therein lies the problem.

We are not encouraged to work on our emotions. We are told to...

Just do it!....Suck it up!.... Feel the fear and do it anyway!... Don't let your feelings get in the way!...

These types of messages often lead people to struggle too hard to reach their goals, to the point where they're either dissatisfied once they've obtained them, or they'll give up along the way.

You are not supposed to agonize towards what you want, but enjoy the ride. Get excited by challenges, rather than feel defeated by them.

We push ourselves because we don't understand the purpose of our emotions.

That's why it is encouraged to be mindful of your emotional states when on the journey to your dreams; being aware of how you feel helps you know whether you are on the path of least resistance, or most tolerant.

We are taught that being focused, determined, dedicated, resourceful, and having a burning desire are the main ingredients in achieving our objectives.

These are much-needed elements, yes.

But they all lose their potency if you are battling with depression. If you get so exhausted, you can't get out of bed.

If your self-esteem doesn't allow you to believe in your potential. Or if your self-confidence cannot rise to the vision of your dreams.

Truth is, you can't get anything done without the right emotions to help you.

Feelings run your business. They run your life! They make your every decision—including the ones you don't make.

Studies show that the more a company cares about the well-being of its employees, the more loyal they are, which saves on turnover rate, position restructuring and training.

Research also demonstrates that companies who have higher employee satisfaction, equally have a higher production rate.

Bottom line: Happy people just perform better.

In my professional experience, employees who take a leave of absence are often those who are burnt out from holding in pent-up negative emotions over time.

Negative emotions such as worry, stress, anxiety, overwhelm, anger, all slow down productivity, communication, and even attendance in the workforce.

This isn't magic; it's science.

Have you ever noticed that when you feel good, it's much easier to focus?

Research shows that when you're in a positive mood, you have more energy.

Your mind is clearer. You're quicker to make decisions and better choices, including for your health: You eat more nutritiously, move your body more, enjoy better night sleeps. When feeling good, you are more socially engaging, personable, more optimistic, see with perspicuity, are more empathetic, and take the time for others.

Conversely, when you're not feeling well, the inner struggle is real.

Your energy is low. It gets harder to focus, and you get more easily distracted. Your mind is not as operative as when you feel positive emotions. You begin to forget things, have greater difficulties remembering, and it gets harder to make those once clear decisions. Uncertainty holds you back, puts things off, and you even start to question your own abilities, and whether this dream of yours is really meant to come true.

Just do it, undoubtedly a catchy slogan, only works for those who are already inspired to pursue their goals.

What does it mean when you think, "I just need to motivate myself"?

It means you need to talk yourself into doing something you don't feel like doing, which is fine now and again, but gets exhausting the more you keep pushing yourself.

That's what happens when employees feel pressed to do something they are not emotionally equipped to do. They end up feeling unsupported, unheard, unseen, and lose faith in themselves and trust in the company they work for.

Plowing through when you're not emotionally ready can lead to disappointment, discouragement, and exhaustion. No one likes to work for a company that gives off the impression that how you feel doesn't matter.

Feelings also drive your marketing.

In fact, marketing is based on resolving your customers' pain points. You sell them on the idea that you can make them feel better (positive emotions) about something that is troubling them (negative emotions).

Your business' success is predicated on your ability to help clients enjoy your products or services and be satisfied working with you.

Truly, you don't have a business unless you can convince people that your product and services will make them feel good.

Whether you are the owner of a company or one of its employees, it is always in the best interest in the success of the company to care about how the workers feel, and create an environment that fosters good mental and emotional health.

Because as you know by now, the better the employees feel, the better service they provide to clients, and the more wins for everyone! If you'd like to find out more, please get in touch with me via trueself-psychology.com

*Rozen, M. (2023) "How Committed Are You to Your New Year Goals?": A Quantitative Study on the Connection of Commitment and Performance with New Year Resolutions. Open Journal of Social Sciences, 11, 415-428. doi: 10.4236/jss.2023.119027.

# Bryan Schaefer

Bryan Schaefer is a Leadership Coach and CAP (Certified Alignment Practitioner). He has over 30 years of experience as a leader, speaker and business owner. He is passionate about helping others and make the world a better place, one leader at a time. He is a compelling story teller and takes what he has learned by doing and presents it in a way that is fun and easy to understand and apply.

As an Alignment Practitioner Bryan helps leaders and teams Master The Art of Alignment. Alignment is what you need to become a Rock Star Leader. Alignment gets everyone's voices heard so the best ideas are implemented. It also creates a truth-telling culture where all team members feel valued and a positive contributor to the process. Alignment evokes a common passion that helps your achieve your mission, vision and goals.

Bryan offers coaching, team building, online courses and keynote speaking through his company Rock Star Leadership Training. www.rockstarleadershiptraining.com

# Chapter 22

# BE AN INCLUSIVE ROCK STAR LEADER AND GET THINGS DONE!

**Bryan Schaefer**

## "Leadership is The Art and Science of Inspiring Commitment and Aligned Action to achieve a clear vision".

Patty Beach—The Art of Alignment, A Practical Guide to Inclusive Leadership.

My name is Bryan Schaefer. I am the founder of Rock Star Leadership Training. I will be accused of overusing the term Rock Star and applying it to Leadership. I come by it honestly from a different perspective, and I will explain why I use it and what it means for me.

## Why Rock Star?

We all love the Superbowl commercials every year. To me, it is the highlight of the game. Did you ever see the Workday Superbowl Ad in 2023? It has actual Rock Stars in the Ad. It started with Paul Stanley from the band KISS saying "Hey corporate types, quit calling yourselves Rock Stars". It also featured Joan Jett, Ozzy Osborne, Gary Clarke Jr. and Billy Idol. It makes the point that when you are "crushing it at work" they call you a rock star. But the real Rock Stars have something to say about that. It is a hilarious take on the overuse of the term. The tag line at the end of the ad says, "Workday, be a finance and HR Rock Star".

I owned a Rock Music School Franchise for 10 years. I had music teachers who were in bands, making music and releasing albums. They were grinding it out, trying to make a living in music and doing what they love. They were also incredible teachers and inspirational to the kids they taught. They were passionate about what they were doing and excited to share their knowledge and love of rock music to the next generation. Not to mention their musical talent when I went to see them perform with their bands. They changed the lives of the kids in the school every day. To me, they were true Rock Stars.

According to Merriam-Webster's Dictionary, a Rock Star is a highly accomplished and well-regarded person in a particular field.

And I want to help you become a Rock Star Leader!

## Change Management—Alignment & Buy-In

As a leader, it is your job to take a company from where you are today to somewhere new and exciting. You must continually evolve, change and grow, or your competition will pass you by. You need to set the direction by inspiring people with a vision of the future that is exciting.

To move things forward and get things done, you must enlist the help of others. You cannot do it alone. Getting your teams onboard, aligned and committed to changes is key to your success as a leader.

I have been involved in many change initiatives in companies of all sizes. From updated IT systems in a large Oil and Gas company, rolling out a new reservation system in an airline and changing the way we teach the instruments at a music school. I have also been affected by change from all different perspectives in my 30+ years in business. As an end user (front-line staff), a leader, a trainer and a business owner.

I have seen millions of dollars wasted on projects that failed. Some that fell short at meeting their intended results. Many projects took longer than expected, were over budget, and did not get the results they had expected. Or did not get the customer satisfaction that was promised.

Here are some shocking statistics:

Source:

https://www.projectmanagementworks.co.uk/project-failure-statistics/

- "Only 64% of projects meet their goals."
- "70% of companies report having at least one failed project in the last year."
- "Organizations lose $109 million for every $1 billion invested in projects and programs."
- "High-performing organizations successfully complete 89% of projects, while low performers only complete 36% successfully. Low performers waste nearly 12 times more resources than high-performing organizations."
- 39% of all projects succeed (delivered on time, on budget, and with required features and functions)
- 43% are challenged (late, over budget, and/or with fewer than the required features and functions) 18% fail (either cancelled before completion or delivered and never used).
- Average % of features delivered – 69%
- Average cost overrun – 59%
- Average time overrun – 74%

**Top 5 reasons projects fail.**

Source: https://www.teamwork.com/blog/project-failure/

1. Not enough resources for the project
2. Poor collaboration and communication
3. Lack of a shared vision on a project
4. Too many modifications to project objectives
5. Poorly planned project cost estimations

There are many reasons projects fail. After seeing these problems time and time again from every vantage point, there is one common denominator: Poor communication, collaboration and vision, which leads to lack of employee engagement and alignment.

Leadership needs to properly align the staff with the changes and get buy-in and commitment at all levels of the organization. To achieve this, you need to become an inclusive leader.

## The Days of Top-Down, command and control leadership is over.

In the past, the leadership model was that all the decisions on the direction of the company were made at the top. This is known as top-down leadership. Decisions were made, without much involvement from people below in the organization. Then those decisions and communication of what needed to be done were cascaded down and people were expected to just march to those orders.

The decision has already been made without consulting those most affected by the change. Then we wonder why we get resistance when we try to implement these changes. It is the job of those on the change management team to get people onboard with the changes. This can include communication plans, town halls, training, support, help desks, office hours, planning software, whatever is required. Trying to convince people this change is a good thing, after the fact.

It is a lot more difficult to get people on board if they were not involved in the decisions up front. They feel undervalued and underappreciated and a "victim" of change, rather than part of it.

Even with the best plans and training programs in place, it may not go smoothly. I was involved in many project roll-outs as a trainer. It was my job to train employees on whatever new technology or processes or systems were being rolled out. You would think people would be excited to be there and happy to learn. Standing at the front of the room, however, sometimes I felt more like I was in the line of fire. Not much training was happening, people took the time to express their discontent with the project as a whole. This was a clear indication that people were not aligned and there was a lack of buy-in and commitment to the changes. They showed resistance to the project, and as a result, things were not moving forward.

What does that look like, and how can we do a better job including more people at all levels of the organization in the change process? There are two benefits of including others in decisions BEFORE they are made;

1. Better Decisions

2. Buy-in, commitment and support — Alignment

**Become an Inclusive Leader**

To be an inclusive leader, you need to seek feedback and ideas from all parts of the organization. Often the people on the frontline (the shop floor), who are most affected by change, have the best perspective. They are also usually closest to the customers. They can provide feedback and talk about what your customers need and how it will impact them.

In larger organizations, you may not be able to get everyone in the company to provide feedback and be involved in all decisions. In these cases, you can appoint representatives from all departments and levels of the organization. They can speak on behalf of their areas of influence. These representatives then take the information back and share the updates with their own teams/departments.

The size of the changes, the number of people affected, and the time you have to work through the decisions will determine how many people you can have in the room. In my training programs with my company, Rock Star Leadership Training, I teach you how to identify stakeholders and determine who should be involved in the initial meetings.

The key is to get as many people as possible involved in the initial discussions. First, get them to agree on the mission, vision, and values. Present the problem or area that needs to be changed, updated, improved and ask the group for ideas on how to solve these challenges.

It is also important to explain why this change is important and how it will help them and the company move forward. Show employees how what we are proposing aligns with our mission, vision, and values. Employees need to know the WHY of a change before they are willing to accept it.

## The Rock Music School Story

I used an inclusive leadership approach with my team when we were rolling out updates to our teaching methods and curriculum at the music school. In this particular situation, the decision about what the changes would be had already happened. This is because it was a franchise and the decision had already come down from corporate.

If school owners and teachers had been engaged up front in the planning process, these changes would have been well received and easier to implement at the school level. The adoption rate system-wide was less than 20%. For most projects, this would not be considered a successful rollout. The way in which these changes were implemented was left to the discretion of each school owner. Many school owners did not have the background in training and change management I had. They struggled to get the adoption and were faced with resistance from staff and students. My school had one of the highest adoption rates in the system because I used a leadership approach to get my teams aligned BEFORE we implemented the changes.

With such a major change that would affect every part of the business, I knew this required a bit more finesse to present the changes to get everyone on board. Before I discussed what the changes were, and what was expected of them, I had a team meeting to level set everyone and make sure we were all on the same page and aligned.

At our team meeting, we discussed what makes our business unique and special. We discussed our mission, vision, and values. I asked team members to tell me (in their own words) why they are passionate about our brand. Then we reviewed our short and long-term goals and where we are going as a company. We were developing a growth mindset, and we talked about what was required to achieve those growth targets. I also asked for feedback and ideas of how we can reach our new goals.

I engaged my staff in conversation about this change, and they felt valued and appreciated and in control of the process. They were given a voice and a chance to express their feelings, about anything, not just the immediate plans. Then I introduced the new tools, technology and curriculum we had to start adopting in our schools. It was much easier for them to accept these changes because I did the work upfront to align them. They understood the WHY of these changes, so they were more willing to accept them. I engaged their hearts, and their minds before they would use their hands (implement the changes). This work should always be done FIRST before you introduce any changes.

You need to create psychological safety in your meetings by allowing everyone to freely and honestly express their concerns with any ideas that are presented. Even the ones coming from the boss.

I love this quote by one of my favorite celebrities, Dwayne "The Rock" Johnson – "Check your ego at the door". To be an inclusive leader, you don't always have to have the best ideas and be right all the time. You also need to be open to feedback and concerns expressed about your ideas, and allow others to come up with good ideas. If you surround yourself with smart, competent, experienced people, you need to allow them to contribute.

As an inclusive leader, you are there to facilitate the process of gathering the best ideas. You sit back and listen, and allow equal participation. This is the only way you can get the truth and the best ideas. If people are afraid to speak up, you will not get the best out of people or honest feedback about the initial proposal.

In my leadership training programs, I teach a systematic approach to presenting proposals, gathering feedback and ideas and reaching agreement. Then the best course of action is approved and everyone has a clear action plan moving forward, and is committed to it.

By creating a culture where all voices matter, and you are free to speak honestly, you will gain trust and credibility as a leader. By asking for feedback and having as many people as possible part of the solutions, you will become an inclusive, Rock Star leader. This will change your culture, and you will start to see the benefit. Buy-in, commitment and support of the changes, plus better decisions. Then going forward, any new ideas, challenges, and changes you are faced with will be well received by everyone. Because you have created a culture of trust and openness that your employees value. The net-net benefit of this leadership approach is better business results.

A study was done, and the findings were published on Effective Leadership Styles on Project Implementation. Renzi T.M. (2020) Open Journal of Leadership 9, 198-213. It stated that, "managers must utilize communication, consultations, and consideration of opinions of team members before decision-making. The collective consultations and considerations are important in successful project implementation because different team members have varied perspectives which in collection form an important source of information from which all team members can learn from".

All the change initiatives that I was involved in that failed, it was because not enough of the people affected by the changes were involved in the initial conversations. This leads to lack of understanding, buy-in, commitment and support. It was not the technology or the systems, or the plan that failed. It was the people who were asked to implement the changes that pushed back.

Lack of commitment, buy-in and alignment can present itself in many different ways. It may not be as direct as an outward expression of deviance. Although in the case of some of my training classes it was. Employees may not be willing to share their concerns with you. Staff begin to feel unappreciated, alienated, helpless and frustrated. Any employee who feels this way will begin to underperform, and eventually leave if the problem is not addressed.

How many projects have you been involved in where frustrations were high and people began to quit because of the way these projects were handled? Or worse, people are getting fired or being blamed for the lack of success of a project. I have seen people get thrown under the bus for projects that failed. The leader did not take ownership or responsibility for the results of the project.

At the end of the day, success of any project stops with you the leader. The way you handle change in your organization will determine whether you are an inclusive leader that people trust and respect, or a leader who uses micro-management and top-down, command and control to lead. Do it, "or else", versus "I am doing it because I want to, and I understand why this is important". That is engagement, buy-in and alignment and gets things done the right way.

In summary, to become a Rock Star Leader you need to do the following things:

- Allow everyone to have a voice and freely express their ideas and opinions.

- Show your employees you value, respect and appreciate them.

- Get everyone aligned to the WHY of a project BEFORE you introduce changes and new ideas.

- To get buy-in and support, include as many people in the organization as possible to contribute feedback and ideas to changes.

- Check your ego at the door.

I am a CAP (Certified Alignment Practitioner) with over 30 years experience in leadership, organizational development and training. I teach leaders how to run alignment meetings and get groups of any size to reach agreements and move towards committed, aligned action. I offer courses, train-the-trainer programs, consulting, coaching and speaking engagements.

If you need help with buy-in, alignment and becoming an inclusive leader, contact me, I would love to work with you. www.rockstarleadershiptraining.com

# Payam Mahmoodi Nia

Following receiving my Ph.D. diploma in 2014, I started working in the semiconductor industry and related research areas. The challenges were technical and not financial, due to Moore's Law and

market demands. Therefore, I learned about designing complex dynamic systems, advanced control systems design methods, data processing, statistics, and machine learning. Completing projects and

winning awards taught me a lot about efficiency and productivity but not without a toll on my mental health. This was a pivotal point for my future plans. Therefore, I decided to launch NextGen

Consulting to share what I learned and to help you to avoid similar struggles. Through NextGen Consulting, we aim to not only solve your challenging problems but also help you and your employees to

manage stress and anxiety with the goal to promote a balanced growth for the businesses and individuals.

SCAN ME

# Chapter 23

# BUSINESS MODEL AND CONTROL SYSTEMS ENGINEERING FUSION FOR MARKET DOMINANCE

**Payam Mahmoodi Nia**

Are you tired of the alarming statistics that reveal the grim reality of business success rates? According to brand expert Bill Schley, a staggering 50% of businesses are doomed to fail right from the start, and only a measly 30% will survive the brutal test of time, living longer than a decade. It's enough to make your head spin and question the sanity of diving into the unpredictable world of entrepreneurship. Imagine a marketplace teeming with aspiring entrepreneurs.

Control systems engineering, a field that harnesses the dynamics of systems, offers a compelling solution. By observing system behavior, processing sensory data, and implementing corrective actions, we can maintain stability in our business processes and achieve deliverables with specific characteristics. The proposal at hand is nothing short of groundbreaking—a precise fusion of control techniques and business management models, capable of achieving systematic success in any market environment. In this chapter, we embark on a journey to unveil the secrets of business management through the lens of control systems engineering, where success is not left to chance.

Let's start by dissecting the thought-provoking quote from the renowned brand expert, Bill Schley. With his keen eye for statistics and probabilities, he paints a vivid picture of the importance of effective business and financial management. Consider this: What if you were aware that your venture only had a 30% chance of success, potentially sacrificing a decade of your precious time and resources? It's a daunting gamble, one where even the roulette table with its reds and blacks seems more forgiving. But here's the alarming truth—it's even worse than you think.

Among the surviving 30%, over 70% of businesses rely on the support of deep-pocketed venture capitalists and government sectors. While they may appear successful on the surface, they are tethered to these sponsors, vulnerable to the whims of a larger crisis. When the storm hits, these businesses are often the first casualties, sacrificed to ensure the survival of the bigger players. By now, it should be abundantly clear how crucial it is to consider models that offer higher potential than the evaluated business success statistics mentioned earlier.

At the core of stability lies a model that establishes a foundation of consistent process flow and financial independence. Achieving these goals is a daunting task for any business, but with the right methodologies and advanced planning, it can be accomplished in the long run. In our exploration of highly productive and profitable companies in the United States, we uncover a critical first step towards stability and independence: business culture and values. As the author emphatically states, "A stable foundation of robust, adaptively maintained culture and values that support stability and independence is a necessary condition to establish dominance in any competitive market."

In this chapter, we delve into the discussion of necessary and sufficient conditions for success in any market. We unravel the key success criteria that transcend industries and unveil the secrets to building a thriving business in any competitive landscape. Brace yourself for a transformative journey where control systems engineering merges with business models, creating a force to be reckoned with. The path to market dominance awaits, and it all starts here.

In order to achieve market success and harness the fusion of business models and control techniques, businesses must execute three main planning schemes that cover the sufficient conditions for triumph. These schemes encompass long-term planning, crisis planning, and post-crisis planning. While the necessary condition of establishing cultural values will be explored in a separate publication, it is crucial to focus on these three planning schemes to ensure market dominance.

To fulfill these planning schemes and guarantee success in the process, management and leaders must invest their time in the following control objectives:

**1. Process Internal and External Stability:** Establishing stability within both internal and external processes is essential. This involves designing systems that can adapt to changes in the business environment while maintaining consistent operational stability.

**2. Parameter Variation Control:** Controlling variations in key parameters is crucial for maintaining operational efficiency. By monitoring and adjusting these parameters, businesses can ensure optimal performance and adaptability in the face of market fluctuations.

**3. Disturbance Rejection and Noise Cancellation:** Businesses must develop strategies to identify and mitigate disturbances that can disrupt operations. Additionally, minimizing noise within the system ensures accurate data processing and decision-making.

It is important to note that each main business function, such as decision-making, financial management, technology development, and application, has its own unique set of processes, parameters, disturbances, and noises that require separate exploration and analysis.

Let's briefly describe the main business functions in order of priority:

**1. CEO (Chief Executive Officer):** Responsible for mainstream decision-making process control.

**2. CFO (Chief Financial Officer):** Manages mainstream financial process control.

**3. CTO (Chief Technical Officer):** Oversees mainstream technology development process control.

**4. CSEO (Chief Systems Engineering Officer):** Coordinates the application of all previous streams in action.

Each operator has a primary control target, along with multiple minor bonus goals that involve considering various variables. While the specifics of each operator's functions and control variables can be explored in a separate discussion, the goal of this chapter is to provide a concise framework of strategies for each operator to satisfy the sufficient conditions for functional stability and performance in any market conditions.

Careful planning by each operator is sufficient to navigate the three inevitable phases of market conditions: stable, unstable, and transient. During stable market conditions, a long-term planning strategy is necessary to maintain business productivity, stability, and independence. Unstable market conditions can trigger crises, requiring a well-thought-out crisis planning approach to navigate these challenging periods. The transient market period follows a crisis, where variables are settling and reforming.

It is important to emphasize that while stable periods in cutting-edge and competitive markets tend to be longer, crisis and post-crisis periods can be relatively shorter. Therefore, a successful business actively plans during stable conditions and proactively prepares for the other two phases. During a crisis, the rate of change of critical business parameters accelerates sharply, highlighting the importance of having a pre-planned strategy in place to tackle market disasters.

By executing these three planning schemes, businesses can position themselves for market dominance and navigate the ever-changing business landscape with confidence.

To ensure stability and success in any market, businesses must implement general functional responsibilities and strategies tailored to each phase or period. It's important to note that these strategies, when combined with the necessary conditions of success, can provide sufficient conditions for achieving dominance. While detailed models and planning for each item will be explored in a future publication, the following provides an overview of the functional responsibilities and strategies for each market phase.

Long-Term Strategies:During stable market conditions, long-term planning plays a vital role. The following action items should be considered:

Generate momentum towards main functional targets: Set clear objectives and work towards achieving them.

Develop ground rules and laws of operation: Establish guidelines and principles that define the path towards the target.

Monitor the process using a reliable feedback system: Implement a feedback mechanism to track progress and identify areas for improvement.

Optimize operation by minimizing noise and disturbance rejection: Streamline processes and minimize external disruptions to maximize efficiency.

Apply corrective control action: Take proactive measures to address any deviations or issues that may arise.

Prediction of possible market and business crises: Anticipate potential crises and develop contingency plans to mitigate their impact.

Strategize planning for possible crisis periods: Prepare strategies and actions to navigate through challenging times.

Crisis Planning: When a crisis hits, businesses need to respond swiftly and effectively. The following steps are crucial:

Analyze crisis cause and effect: Understand the root causes and consequences of the crisis to formulate an appropriate response.

Evaluate previously prepared crisis planning: Assess the effectiveness of existing crisis plans and identify areas for improvement.

Revise crisis planning and prepare to adapt: Adjust crisis strategies based on lessons learned and changing market conditions.

Actuate crisis strategy: Implement the revised crisis plan to address the challenges at hand.

Monitor the effectiveness of crisis management strategy: Continuously evaluate the effectiveness of the crisis response and make necessary adjustments based on market changes.

Strategize planning for the post-crisis period: Develop strategies to transition from crisis mode to a stable period.

Post-Crisis Planning: As the market stabilizes after a crisis, businesses need to regroup and plan for the future.

The following steps are essential:

- Evaluate functional parameters and confirm the crisis is over: Assess the impact of the crisis on various functional aspects of the business and ensure stability has been restored.

- Generate crisis lessons learned material: Document and analyze the lessons learned from the crisis to avoid similar pitfalls.

- Strategize the next long-term (stable) period

- Monitor the phase change towards a stable period

- Define the transition process to the stable period

It's important to customize the action items for each phase based on the specific business deliverables and functional objectives of each operator. Success at each level of operation depends on optimizing several parameters, and finding optimal solutions to these parameters can drive over-all success.

In addition to the above phases, a key elemental require-ment for achieving dominance in any market is the asso-ciation of a business's product with defined quality levels and cost. The optimization of this relationship is crucial. While the highest quality product tends to have a higher cost, finding the optimal balance is essential. The advan-tages of a quality product are numerous, while the disad-vantage lies in its cost. The key to achieving dominance lies in producing the highest quality product with the lowest cost. However, it's crucial to note that maintain-ing and protecting the quality and cost of a released prod-uct throughout its lifecycle is even more critical than the initial release cost and quality. Consistently maintaining product quality and cost will ensure long-term competi-tiveness and attractiveness to customers, leading to busi-ness stability and robustness in the face of market fluctua-tions.

Remember, while these strategies provide a general frame-work, detailed analysis and further investigation are need-ed to create a comprehensive plan tailored to each specific business and market environment.

In addition to considering the relationship between qual-ity and cost, it is crucial to examine how quality relates to defined product application and use case duration. Match-ing the right quality level to specific use cases is essential. We wouldn't use silk gloves to wash dishes, nor would we want to wear low-cost synthetic polymer underwear. Care-ful consideration of product use cases and durations is necessary to define the appropriate quality and cost range. Quality should always be a priority, with cost and other product aspects considered secondary. It is my respon-sibility to emphasize the importance of quality and its impact on customers and the environment. Let's expand the discussion on this topic and explore some of the main advantages of investing in quality for both businesses and customers.

- **Financial Stability in Any Market:** Maintaining a high-quality product over the long run generates sufficient internal and external revenue, creating systematic business stability in any market condition.

- **Employee Satisfaction:** A product backed by quality reduces tension in the workplace, builds trust across all levels, and aligns stakeholders, fostering overall internal harmony and job satisfaction.

- **Waste Reduction and Higher Yield:** Quality-focused design and production processes from the outset result in waste reduction and higher yield. Though the initial cost may be higher, it creates a strong foundation for return on investment over time.

- **Reduced Downtime and Maintenance Costs:** Investing in quality minimizes monitoring and control costs, reduces resources and time spent on maintenance and troubleshooting, and minimizes systematic downtime in a product's lifecycle.

- **Creating a Competitive and Healthy Market:** A healthy and competitive market flourishes when businesses exceed customer expectations, providing satisfaction through high-quality products. Quality is the foundation of a thriving market.

- **Increasing Customer Knowledge Base:** A market driven by competition for high-quality products boosts awareness, knowledge, and development capabilities—essential elements for market stability and robustness.

- **Improving Customer Mental and Physical Health:** Reducing waste and downtime through quality products builds trust, decreases the need for returns and troubleshooting, and minimizes potential health and financial issues for customers. A healthy customer is a necessary condition for a stable market.

- **Reducing Harmful Environmental Impact:** Minimizing excessive production and use resulting from low-quality products stabilizes availability and demand in the market. This creates a chain reaction, reducing energy consumption, waste generation, and environmental impact, contributing to a healthier planet.

## Final Notes on the Importance of Quality

High-quality product development leads to customer satisfaction and triggers a cascade of benefits for the market, social well-being, and long-term cost reduction. However, achieving this requires a social and cultural revolution that empowers quality product development and educates consumers about the benefits of investing in quality. In many societies today, lower- and middle-class customers prioritize cost reduction over finding the balance between quality and cost for their everyday needs. This has allowed some businesses in the past to thrive by producing low-quality, extremely low-priced products and services. However, it has become evident over time that such practices lack respect for human well-being, global welfare, and environmental rights. Low-quality products generate minimal profits for their producers while causing disastrous waste generation, high consumption rates, and significant damage to nature and its inhabitants.

Consider this: Imagine investing a thousand dollars in a pair of shoes that will last you a decade, providing comfort and keeping your feet healthy. Now compare that to spending fifty bucks every year on two low-quality shoes that offer poor materials and design. The former promotes confidence, mental well-being, generates less waste, and respects your main natural wealth—your physical health.

The latter, on the other hand, does the opposite. To my perspective, wearing shoes made from leaves and twigs is healthier, more cost-effective, and more respectful than using low-quality, damaging shoes. I leave it to the reader to judge and plan for a personal revolution in behavior and decision-making.

Investing in quality also brings about environmental benefits. By producing durable and long-lasting products, businesses contribute to waste reduction. Such products require fewer replacements, resulting in less material consumption and reduced waste generation. Moreover, the emphasis on quality encourages companies to adopt sustainable practices throughout the production process. This includes utilizing eco-friendly materials, optimizing energy efficiency, and minimizing carbon emissions. By reducing their ecological footprint, businesses can become leaders in environmental stewardship and inspire others to follow suit.

For consumers, the advantages of quality are manifold. High-quality products deliver superior performance, durability, and reliability, enhancing customer satisfaction. They provide peace of mind, knowing that their investment will endure and meet their expectations. Furthermore, the longevity of quality products reduces the need for frequent replacements, resulting in cost savings over time. Customers also benefit from reduced maintenance and repair costs, as well as minimized downtime. This allows them to focus on their priorities without disruptions caused by faulty or unreliable products.

Embracing quality as a fundamental value paves the way for a brighter future, where excellence and sustainability coexist harmoniously.

# Jacqueline Vrba

Guatemalan entrepreneur Jacqueline Vrba, residing in the US since 2014, founded BIOME Herbolaria, specializing in natural herbal products. Her venture spurred interest from inspired women leading her to take action.

Recognizing the need for accessible trade training, she established the Fridars Institute in California in 2019, empowering women to build businesses. Having served 4,000+ students, the institute offers education in business and marketing, guided by Jacqueline's expertise.

With a mission to ensure women have an outlet to find their passion and generate income, she's fueled by the adversity she faced growing up in a third world country, experiencing a lack of educational resources all while enduring economical and personal hardship.

Jacqueline continues to find ways to uplift her community through events promoting personal growth and self-love. She also continuously furthers her education, having achieved a certification with John Maxwell and seeking education from renowned mentors.

SCAN ME

# Chapter 24

# OVERCOMING SHAME AND EMBRACING EMPOWERMENT

**Jacqueline Vrba**

## *"Turn your pivotal moments into bridges to success."*

Jacqueline Vrba

As I begin this chapter, I grapple with what more could be said after renowned Brian Tracy's extensive work on overcoming fears and habits. The self-doubt accompanying this writing process unveiled a realization: a lack of self-love contributes to my fear. I decided to confront it head-on, acknowledging it first and then declaring, one of the affirmations I repeat daily, "I Trust Myself!" despite my fears.

Let me tell you a bit about myself. I am a successful woman, an entrepreneur with a life that many people might consider very fortunate. I make good money, have a good business, and have a handsome husband (at least in my eyes) who makes the world's best coffee and cooks delicious meals. I have three beautiful children aged 6 and 9, and 20, the latter being my beautiful, smart, daughter who is also my right-hand person. We are a normal family, which means we sometimes disagree on things but know how to come to compromises.

In my professional field, I am the Founder and Director of an Institute in California, where we've guided over 4,000 students to start new businesses or learn a trade. Most people would say my life is enviable, but it wasn't always like this. Let me share a part of my story and how I am one of those people who were not fortunate at birth, since I was born within and grew up in shame.

### Shame Passed Down from the Womb

I was born into adversity, without promising statistics on my side. My first experience with shame began in my mother's womb. This shame was formed because my mother knew she would give birth to a child without a father. Imagine the shame a woman felt in the 1980s when she realized that the person who impregnated her would not take responsibility for the child. The shame of telling her family and siblings. Even more painful, a realization that I didn't analyze at the time, but came to understand approximately five years ago when I recalled a conversation with my late mother. She said to me, "Nena" (that's what she called me), "I told him I didn't want it, but he didn't listen" (referring to my father). She even cried, but he still didn't listen. Years later, I realized that I was a product of rape, and although my mother never used those words, it was a fact. To this day, I believe it was her love for me that made her choose not to see it that way.

## Shame of Poverty

Don't get me wrong; I never expected to be born in Buckingham Palace, but if you've never grown up in poverty, you might not fully understand how tough it can be. I heard thousands of times that we were poor, my family would say, "Hijita, we are poor." The shame and guilt associated with the feeling of being poor became instilled in my brain. Yet, as an adult, I reevaluate these perceptions and recognize that poverty is a state of mind, not an inherent flaw to be ashamed of.

I know it's not easy to break free from that mindset because we don't have the mentality to prepare ourselves and change our habits. We are filled with fears and invisible family legacies that we don't want to change to avoid upsetting our clan, including the victim mentality that keeps us from taking action.

## Shame of Having an Alcoholic, and Drug-Addicted Mother

My mother taught me a lot. Please don't judge her after the harsh words I used to describe her. I'm sure she came into this world to support me, so I could have the growth I've had. But I do remember vividly all the difficult things my mother went through. She was raped by a gang, attempted suicide many times; it was like an endless nightmare week after week. I always had it on my mind, "and now what is she going to do?" It was like living day and night, week after week and month after month in a never-ending nightmare. Some weeks she spent in jail, other days she was fighting with the neighbors, or with members of our own family, her own children, stealing money to get what she thought would satiate her, or some days she'd disappear altogether, and left people looking for her. The shame of living with that, I let that begin to overpower me because people referred to me as the daughter of the drug addict.

## Shame of Becoming What You Despise

I was barely managing to finish high school. I struggled with judging my mother because I couldn't understand why she didn't reach for more inner strength. I couldn't grasp the reality that despite her children needing her, she didn't try hard enough to find a way out. I remember so clearly, I begged her, in tears, when my first brother was born to please stop damaging herself, to please stop putting my baby brother in danger, to wake up and see that we, her children, need her. This was just before I started high school, my uncle left the house, I begged him not to, in tears, it was many moments like these that began to eat at me, that filled me with shame.

However, not once did it even occur to me to stop going to school, it was in my mind my only escape, to get an education. Despite all that was going on at home, I went on to high school because my uncle had the generosity to pay for it. To this day, I love him and feel so grateful for that gesture.

However, through high school, I began to hate her, hate the shame that she had shackled me to. Some days I really hated her, but all that hate was like projecting itself in a mirror, and it began to bounce back and then, without noticing, I was gradually becoming like her. I was seeking refuge in friendships that were equally lost and confused.

## Shame of Not Having the Power to Say NO

I remember one night at a bar with some friends; I was exhausted because I had been going out for three consecutive nights. That last night, I didn't want to go out, but I went anyway. I went to the bathroom and realized that I had no willpower. I was in a place I didn't want to be because I wanted to be accepted and loved. At that moment, a thought came to me: "This is what your mother felt." She was still alive at the time, and I burst into tears. I prayed to God in that place that I wouldn't kill myself, but if that was my destiny, I wanted Him to take my life. As I cried, I truly felt it in my heart. I believe that night, He heard me. Gradually, I began standing up to my friends and started having different thoughts.

I started surrounding myself with things that were going to bring the right kind of people my way, I stopped focusing on the shame that was my life, and started focusing on the decisions I could make that would make my life a better one, despite my shortcomings growing up.

## The Impact of Making Powerful Decisions

### First Powerful Decision

One of the decisions I made was based on something I heard on the radio – that computers were the future, and I should study them. At the time, I must have been around 19 years old (I don't remember well). I lived two hours away from the computer school. Oh, I forgot to mention, I grew up in my grandmother's house, but we lost it, and we were homeless for several years. When we finally got a house, it was far from the city. It was the only place I could afford, and luckily, it was a good place. It was two hours away, but I was determined. Even if it meant a four-hour round trip on a bus that was honestly quite scary to board, I did it. I completed my Computer Technician course, and because education always pays well, years later, that knowledge helped me get a job. I was chosen over excellent candidates with university degrees because I excelled in computer skills. I got a job at a wonderful company, and thanks to them, or rather, thanks to that job opportunity, I got my first visa and came to know the USA.

## Second Powerful Decision

Finding the "how" instead of dwelling on the "why"? When we are young or simply lack guidance or role models, we often feel lost in limbo. We desire things but don't know how to achieve them, and we get stuck in the "why." The "why" is a need to understand the role of being a victim that we put on ourselves or that others have imposed on us. We become so focused on complaining that we forget to think about how to solve the problem.

Do you remember me telling you that I was homeless as a child? Well, I decided that I wouldn't suffer from that again, and my goal, driven by one of my greatest fears, was to have a home, a house of my own. I remember thinking that I didn't care how far away it might be; I wanted my own house. So, when I'm old, maybe I won't have money to eat, but I'll have my home. Because with a home, I can have a simple meal and still be okay. The truth is, what I was seeking was stability, that security I couldn't receive as a child.

Let me tell you what I did. I had three jobs in a day: Secretary from 10 am to 5 pm, Hostess at a restaurant from 8 pm to 12 am, and working at the Airport from 4 am to 6 am. I didn't last long in this hustle, as my hair started falling out, and I was constantly exhausted. I realized that this wasn't the path I needed to take. I needed a job where I could earn more, and that's when I started asking myself, "How can I get a higher-paying job?"

I looked in the newspaper for job listings with the best salaries, and there were two options – one in sales and the other, well, let's just say it's better left unsaid. You can probably imagine. At the time, those jobs required something I didn't have: a car, and not just any car, but a recent model. I didn't even know how to drive, but I thought, "I can learn." The rest of the story is history, as you can imagine. I saved up enough money, bought my first car, and started working in sales. I worked diligently, with faith, and I educated myself in sales. I read several books, and I succeeded. Instead of living in the victim mentality and asking, "Why me?" I asked myself a simple question: "How can I achieve this according to my capabilities and without killing myself in the process?"

## Believing in Yourself Regardless of the Outcomes

I remember my first daughter, Rebecca, studying in a nearby school. It wasn't a public school, but I wasn't satisfied because some girls there were really rude, and I wanted something better for my daughter. I wasn't happy with the quality of education she was receiving, as she was being mistreated. Now I believe the law of attraction and faith go hand in hand, and I firmly believe that when you have faith in yourself, you automatically have faith in others, including my daughter. My 3rd Powerful decision in this chapter that changed my life was when I saw an opportunity in an advertisement for a scholarship at one of the best schools in Guatemala.

Despite doubts and the fear of rejection, I decided to take the first step and submit my daughter's grades, and we passed the initial phase.

Imagine this: in the first on-site test, there were over 500 children; honestly, I thought they wouldn't call us, but they did. My daughter passed. Throughout this time, I didn't want to demoralize her if she didn't get it, I wanted her to feel that it mattered, but if not, we would try again the next year. After three tests and overcoming some obstacles, I remember, in the final test, my car broke down. I recall taking a taxi, and it turned out to be one of the best decisions of my life; she was awarded the scholarship. This achievement was not just a triumph for her, but also a door that opened for me to a new dimension of possibilities. That school was attended by the best families and even the children of former presidents of Guatemala. I couldn't believe it. I remember the first day I entered there after knowing she was accepted; I sat in front of the soccer fields and cried. I didn't want anyone to see me cry, but tears of gratitude flowed because I knew this was the best education for my daughter.

## "Turning Shame into an Advantage"

At the American school where my daughter received her scholarship, I faced the shame of not fully understanding English during meetings. On one occasion, my pivotal moment was being in a meeting, they asked a question, and I wasn't sure whether to raise my hand or not; honestly, in the end, I did raise it, but I felt powerless instead of empowered.

I decided to turn that shame into a catalyst for self-improvement by enrolling in English classes for a year. This decision not only allowed me to regain my power but also opened countless doors, even in the realm of love, as my current husband doesn't speak Spanish. Learning English became an empowering and connecting tool; true empowerment comes from preparation, so never stop learning.

## "Overcoming Economic Adversity"

I remember a time when my family's financial situation was precarious. Every day was a struggle for survival, and the idea of a better future seemed like a distant illusion. However, instead of succumbing to despair, I saw this adversity as a challenge to overcome. I began seeking higher-paying job opportunities, educating myself in computer skills at INTECAP, studying personal finances, and making smarter decisions regarding expenses and investments. This period of financial hardship transformed into an intensive course in resilience and financial management, teaching me valuable lessons that I apply to this day.

## "Transforming Loss into a Learning Moment"

The loss of a loved one is a devastating blow, a moment that seems to halt time and plunge us into a pit of grief. However, after losing a close family member, my mother, I decided to channel my grief into something that would honor her memory. It wasn't immediate; it took me over ten years to heal, and I still miss her. Instead of carrying the shame I often felt for being the daughter of an addict, I decided to change all that energy into something wonderful and positive, supporting families so they wouldn't go through the same ordeal. Fridars Institute opened its doors on March 7, 2020, dedicated to helping women find their purpose and awaken their passion. Fridars Institute transformed my perspective on death and the legacy each of us can leave behind. I am a witness to my mother's suffering, as she wanted to change but didn't know how. Seeing her suffer and ultimately pass away due to emotional problems, those sadnesses (addictions) that often go unnoticed in the Latino community, motivated me to create something positive, and help families avoid that path. At Fridars Institute, we have assisted over 4,000 women in achieving their dreams through our training and courses.

## A Negative Example: The Misused "Trigger" Moment

Now, I want to share a negative example. Imagine a moment in your life where, instead of facing a challenge, you allow fear and negativity to dominate you. This destructive approach not only harms you, but those around you as well. It's crucial to recognize these moments and learn how to redirect them in a positive direction.

## Education as a Transformative Power

Witnessing the transformative power of education and how it changes lives, I was inspired to found Fridars Institute in California. Can you see how self-improvement and education can change lives? Fridars Institute serves the community by changing lives through careers that promote personal growth and development. Scientific studies support the idea that education not only enriches individuals but also enhances society as a whole. One of Fridars Institute's mottos is "An Empowered Woman Empowers Her Children," and this is a requirement in society: empowered children.

Education is a powerful tool that allows us to cross bridges to brighter futures, overcoming obstacles and turning challenging moments into opportunities for growth.

# Photos Copyrights Information